S. SEKOU ABODU

CW00493584

Sho & Mo
Loaded: Empowered.
Sekoudodo
London 2015

PRAYERNOMICS

BECOMING STRONG PRAYER ECONOMIES

PRAYERNOMICS

Becoming strong prayer economies

Sekou Publishing
sekou@sekou.me

Copyright © 2015 by Sekou Abodunrin

Cover Design and Page Layout
Kenteba Kreations
www.kentebakreations.com

ISBN: 978-0-9575677-5-7

Published by Sekou Publishing. All rights reserved.

No part of this book may be reproduced in any form, by photocopying or by any electronic or mechanical means, including information storage or retrieval systems, without permission in writing from both the copyright owner and publisher of this book.

Unless otherwise indicated, all Scripture quotations are taken from the King James Version of the Bible.

Scripture quotations marked (MONTGOMERY) are taken from The Centenary Translation of the New Testament by Helen Barrett Montgomery. Copyright © 1924 by the American Baptist Publication Society.

Scripture quotations marked (GOODSPEED) are taken from The New Testament: An American Translation by Edgar J. Goodspeed (Copyright © 1923, 1948 by the University of Chicago)

Scripture quotations marked (AMPLIFIED) are taken from the Amplified® Bible, Copyright © 1954, 1958, 1962, 1964, 1965, 1987 by The Lockman Foundation. Used by permission. www.lockman.org
Scripture quotations marked (MIRROR) are taken from MIRROR BIBLE. Copyright © 2012

Scripture quotations marked (SAWYER) are taken from The New Testament Translated From the Original Greek by Leicester Ambrose Sawyer (Copyright © 1858 Boston)

The author has emphasized some words in Scripture quotations in bold type.

Pondering redemption realities is your head gear that protects your mind; then give voice to the Word of God, this is your spiritual sword. Prevail in persistent prayer; praying in the spirit includes every form of prayer, whether it be a prayer of request or a prayer of thanksgiving and worship or interceding for the saints, don't do all the talking, always be attentive to the voice of the spirit. (Prayer is so much more than a one way conversation.)

Ephesians 6:17-18 (MIRROR)

CONTENTS

INTRODUCTION

The fact that you have picked up this book tells me it was worth writing it. Perhaps someone thrust it on your hands thinking you needed a crash course on prayer or maybe you had time on your hands and needed to kill the boredom and the universe contrived to randomly drop this book on your laps. Even if you plan to underline all the bits that you do not agree with, that's ok by me. We are now on this adventure together. Yay!

For whatever reason that you find yourself reading this book ...

This book is for you.

I am glad you are reading it. Thank you.

In it you will find the blazing-hot devouring fire of God's love burning up your fears and reminding you to pray like God's righteous one. You'll find answers about prayer and those answers will open up the Pandora's box of many more tough questions. If the book is not simple or clear enough, we will do a better job next time.

I will not confirm any suspicions that you have about your being a sinner in the hands of an angry God. No, we will not be on that kind of journey in this book. Hopefully you'll awaken to the sacrifices of Christ that have made you a bona fide saint in the company of a happy God. Pray because the ferocious love of God has devoured your sense of condemnation and conversing with God becomes a joy.

On a subliminal level, this book aims to speak to you the language of heroic love in the heart of Jesus that caused Him to erect a throne of grace to which we can boldly come. I write in hope that this could awaken in you the reality of Jesus as the strongest obsession of your life.

The message in the book is an unapologetic celebration of Jesus as victor. He alone is our victory. We pray from that victory which keeps on giving.

God has given us different types of prayers for a reason. Think of them as keys that open different doors. One thing is sure, if we use the correct key, no matter how big the door, it will open. God gave us different types of prayers because He wants us to be able to receive from Him no matter where we find ourselves in our spiritual journey.

Moreover He is aware that we are each at different levels of spiritual development. He also knows that we each receive better through certain types of prayers than we do through other types of prayers. A number of these prayers work together. We should avail ourselves of all of them.

We must remain students of the Word and prayer. Stay curious, stay teachable, keep receiving answers and never stop asking questions.

APPRECIATION

We learn from those who have gone before us. I appreciate those teachers on whose shoulders I stand, and who have put in the hard work required to simplify complexity.

To my wonderful wife and intoxicant – Olatundun Oyeteju.

1

PRAYER DEFINED

Why pray

It was the Apostle James, who said,

> *If any of you lack wisdom, let him ask of God, that giveth to all men*
> *liberally, and upbraideth not; and it shall be given him.*
> *James 1:5*

Notice that James does not just tell the believer to pray to God. He specifically says to pray to God who gives to all men.

The Spirit would have us understand a fundamental principle: The most important fact about prayer is not the size or complexity of our need but the understanding of God's true nature. When we pray, we often project our own images of rejection, unworthiness and refusal onto God and we anticipate that because of some failing or blemish, God is going to scream a resounding "no" from the throne. As we feed on God's Word,

God's Word dismantles our false ideas about God and removes the fog that hinders us from seeing God clearly for who He is. See God clearly, and then pray boldly from what you see in Him.

If prayer is the key, then the revelation of God's love is the master key that unlocks the prayer key. James' logic is that we ask in prayer because He gives.

Everything that God does He does because of His love. He does not give to us because of what we do but because of who He is. God is love; therefore He is a giver who gives liberally.

That is the foundation of prayer.

The logic is that the grace of God teaches us to pray boldly.

The Apostle Paul through whom the Lord Jesus gave to His Church the revelation of God's grace wrote extensively about God's grace and instructed the Church to pray without ceasing.

Jesus, who was the embodiment of God's grace, often prayed all night.

In prayer, we come boldly to the throne of grace (See Heb. 4:16). You see, it is not the throne of how-I-have-lived-my-life, the throne of I-am-not-good-enough nor is it even the throne of I-have-earned-this-answer. It is the throne of grace.

When you come, God does not see lousy sinner. He sees His own. He sees the precious fruit of the earth made worthy by the redemption that is in Christ Jesus. Is that what you see?

God has erected a throne on which grace sits in majesty and from which the entire blessing flows richly, freely and without any accusation from God.

At the throne of grace we find mercy and grace to help. Mercy means you will not get the "mess" that you deserve, whatever you think that mess is. Grace means you will get what Jesus deserves. He qualifies you.

Thus prayer and the grace of God go hand in hand on earth.

Since God is a giver, why does He not just do whatever He wants to whenever it pleases Him on the earth?

That is an important question.

Our prayer does not pressure God to give. God works through our prayer because of the way that He has set up the earth.

The heaven, even the heavens, are the Lord's: but the earth hath he given to the children of men.
Psalm 115:16

And God said, Let us make man in our image, after our likeness: and let them have dominion over the fish of the sea, and over the fowl of the air, and over the cattle, and over all the earth, and over every creeping thing that creepeth upon the earth.
Genesis 1:26

As far as we can see in God's Word, it was God's pleasure to give the earth to His man. Man had no conditions to fulfill except to exercise that dominion.

Pay close attention to what God said. God did not give a portion of the earth to man nor did He give most of it to man. God told man to have dominion **over all the earth.** This means that by God's design, we bring Him maximum pleasure by exerting this God-given dominion over all the earth.

This dominion over all the earth is a lease that will expire. For as long as that lease is in effect all the earth belongs to man. This is a staggering fact if you think about it. God has trusted man with a dominion that covers the whole earth and He did not attach any conditions to it!

The implication of this far-reaching dominion that God gave to man is that God needs a human being in order for God to be able to legally bring about change on the earth. God is not sharing the regency of the earth with man. God has made man the regent of the earth. It is implied that God needs man in order to bring His influence into the earth when God gave unconditional dominion over all the earth to man.

We are the ones that authorize and release the power that is required to get the job done on earth!

God is mindful of what He said in Genesis concerning man's dominion on the earth. He acts within the parameters of man's dominion. Not understanding this, many people with the best intention in the world, expect God to do whatsoever He pleases on the earth. They scratch their heads when God does not appear to stage a "coup" and take over the affairs of their lives as well as that of the whole earth. Unconsciously they are robbing God of maximizing the pleasure of seeing His men rise up in dominion over all and any issue of life.

Concerning God's character, God gave the Psalmist a revelation that shows us what God is like. He inspired the psalmist to say,

I will worship toward thy holy temple, and praise thy name for thy lovingkindness and for thy truth: for thou hast magnified thy word above all thy name.
Psalm 138:2

You need to understand that to the Hebrew mind; a name is not just what you call a thing. A name expresses the nature of a thing. That expression, "thy name" should translate in our western mindset to "your very self". Therefore what God is showing the Psalmist is that God has subjected Himself to His own Word. Since God by His own Word gave the earth to man, God needs man to authorise Him in order for God to legally influence the earth. This in a nutshell is why we pray. Prayer provides a legal cover for God's activity on the earth.

Without our words either spoken or prayed, God's legal access on the earth is zero.

What is prayer?

Prayer is supernatural communion between the spirit of man on the earth and the Spirit of God in the spirit dimension through our speaking to God the Word He gave to us. We speak these words to God with our mouth and our thoughts as our heart ponders on His Word. This is intimacy of the highest order. It brings pleasure to both the Spirit of God and the human spirit.

Prayer is a divine exchange where we send words and thoughts towards God who also injects His Word and His thoughts into our thoughts. This fulfills God's heart-cry and hunger for fellowship with His man.

As our hearts keep thinking on the thoughts that He has given us, God gets the opportunity to use our heart to give us corresponding actions. It is this combination of prayer, words, thoughts and corresponding actions that manifests our prayers on the earth.

Prayer is this two-way communion involving the combination of words, thoughts and actions.

Heart-Mouth combination

A good man out of the good treasure of his heart bringeth forth that which is good; and an evil man out of the evil treasure of his heart bringeth forth that which is evil: for of the abundance of the heart his mouth speaketh.
Luke 6:45

According to the bible, the heart and mouth of both good men and evil men work on the same principles. It is not one set of rules for the heart of good men and another set for that of evil men. One of those laws is that we bring treasures out of our heart through our own mouth.

You could flip that principle on its head and say that we deposit treasures into the heart though the mouth also.

The principle is that whatever your heart is filled with will come out of your own mouth whether the content is good or bad. This principle shows that the heart of a man is connected to his mouth. Your heart will release the power of any treasure that is placed within it.

Based on this law we understand that whatever we speak out of our own mouths long enough gets embedded into our heart.

The life-giving Word of God is the purest spiritual treasure that there is.

When we make it a habit to speak God's Word, God's Word

ultimately penetrates and lodges itself in our hearts. Our heart then releases the power locked within the Word that is planted within it. In this way, scriptural prayer unlocks and supplies tremendous spiritual power (See James 5:16).

It is this tremendous power supplied through our speaking, praying and thinking the Word that God uses to accomplish His will on the earth.

You must realize that God does not bring His will to pass on the earth just because He is God. If His will comes to pass just because He is God, then nothing but His will can happen on the earth. It is a solemn truth that since God has given the earth to men, God uses the heart of men to supply the power that is required for His will to get done on earth.

If we do not supply this power in prayer the will of God remains unfulfilled. Without men agreeing with God by speaking, thinking and praying His Word, the spiritual treasure does not enter into their hearts therefore God's will remains undone. The will of God therefore does not come to pass on the earth.

God needs you!

Hey! There is resistance

Prayer is a two-way intimate communion between God's Spirit and the human spirit. Through prayer God is reproducing heaven on earth through the human heart.

Though prayer is communion between God's Spirit and man's spirit, man is not only exclusively allowing God's thoughts into his heart. Since man sometimes cooperates with the thoughts of satan the deceiver, other forces are unleashed on the earth.

There is warfare involved in receiving manifestation for the prayers that we have prayed. This is because men also permit other spirit beings to influence our heart and through our heart gain a foothold in our world.

In God's Word we catch glimpses of the fact that there is resistance to manifestation of answers to prayer. This fact is brought forth as we examine the prayers of Daniel.

Consider the following,

> *Then said he unto me, Fear not, Daniel: for from the first day that thou didst set thine heart to understand, and to chasten thyself before thy God, thy words were heard, and I am come for thy words. But the prince of the kingdom of Persia withstood me one and twenty days: but, lo, Michael, one of the chief princes, came to help me; and I remained there with the kings of Persia. Now I am come to make thee understand what shall befall thy people in the latter days: for yet the vision is for many days.*
> *Daniel 10:12-14*

The angel Gabriel shows Daniel in clear terms that there are other spirits who want to hinder Daniel's prayer.

In addition the Apostle Paul tells the believer the following,

> *(For the weapons of our warfare are not carnal, but mighty through God to the pulling down of strong holds;) Casting down imaginations, and every high thing that exalteth itself against the knowledge of God, and bringing into captivity every thought to the obedience of Christ;*
> *2 Corinthians 10:4-5*

As we read this we must remember that though there are spirits that try to hinder manifestation, they are limited to the permission that men give them. You see, in much the same way that God is subject to man's dominion, these spirit beings are still subject to the fact that man is the authorizing agent on the earth. In order for these spirits to mount a successful resistance, they must plant their thoughts and ideas into the heart of a man.

These spirits cannot attack God's Spirit or the recreated human spirit. They set their war machine against the human heart.

This spiritual warfare registers as thoughts seeking access to our hearts. The heart of man is so important that both good and bad spirit beings need the heart of man in order to hasten or delay the performance of God's will on the earth.

If we do not take certain thoughts captive, those thoughts will redirect the power released through prayer. Thus we do not only see satan mounting resistance, the Word teaches us that he will try to abuse that power through imaginations that are contrary to God's Word.

The pivotal nature of the human heart is showcased in the scripture below,

Let them not depart from thine eyes; keep them in the midst of thine heart. For they are life unto those that find them, and health to all their flesh. Keep thy heart with all diligence; for out of it are the issues of life.
Proverbs 4:21-23

The startling thing about your heart is that it will accommodate and produce more of whatever you keep within it – whether good or bad! In fact the human heart will produce bad thoughts planted within it just as efficiently as it would produce good thoughts.

A stronghold is a way of keeping and protecting thoughts and ideas within the human heart. It does not matter whether these ideas are good or bad. There is no morality to this. It works irrespective of morals.

Though prayer is between God and man, man has to use the peace of God to protect his heart from other spirit beings who want to hijack the power of the heart of man.

This concept of resistance and redirection to our prayers is further illustrated in the account of the temptation of the Lord Jesus.

And Jesus being full of the Holy Ghost returned from Jordan, and was led by the Spirit into the wilderness, Being forty days tempted of the devil. And in those days he did eat nothing: and when they were ended, he afterward hungered. And the devil said unto him, If thou be the Son of God, command this stone that it be made bread. And Jesus answered him, saying, It is written, That man shall not live by bread alone, but by every word of God. And the devil, taking him up into an high mountain, shewed unto him all the kingdoms of the world in a moment of time. And he brought him to Jerusalem, and set him on a pinnacle of the temple, and said unto him, If thou be the Son of God, cast thyself down from hence:
Luke 4:1-5,9

Jesus fasted and prayed in the wilderness by the leading of the Holy Spirit. Since the prayer of the righteous makes tremendous power available, the Lord Jesus must have supplied tremendous power as a result of this time of prayer and fasting!

It was after His 40-day fast that the Devil tempted Jesus in the wilderness. He wanted to redirect that power that Jesus had made available!

It was while Jesus was physically standing in the wilderness that He was taken up the temple at Jerusalem. If we are not careful we take that to mean that Jesus was also physically present at Jerusalem. If you had been in the Jerusalem Temple on that day, you would not have seen any man standing on its pinnacle. As a man Jesus could not physically be in the wilderness and Jerusalem simultaneously. His humanity means that He can only be in one place at one time. The implication is that the temptation of Jesus was exactly like our temptation today – it happened in His thought realm just like we also get tempted through thoughts and imaginations.

In addition we are told that satan led Jesus up a mountain and showed Him all the kingdoms of the world in a moment of time. This mountain could not have been a physical mountain. Even today, in the Middle East, there is no single mountain from which you can see all the kingdoms of the earth at once. This buttresses the fact that the temptation happened in Jesus' thought realm.

The devil was able to stir up all this temptations even after 40 days of fasting! This must mean that fasting and prayer, even for 40 days, do not keep the devil away nor do they stop temptations from coming. If the Lord Jesus could not stop the devil from coming to Him after 40 days fasting, neither will you be able to.

It does not matter whether the devil comes or not. What matters is what is kept in your heart.

The Word of God does not keep us in the dark concerning how temptation works.

Let no man say when he is tempted, I am tempted of God: for God cannot be tempted with evil, neither tempteth he any man: But every man is tempted, when he is drawn away of his own lust, and enticed. Then when lust hath conceived, it bringeth forth sin: and sin, when it is finished, bringeth forth death.
James 5:13-15

James teaches us that every man is tempted through his own lusts. Lust simply means strong desires. The fact that the Lord Jesus could be tempted is clear proof of his humanity. It also shows that temptation is not a sin. The Lord Jesus was a bona fide man who was tempted like we are (See Heb. 4:15). This means He also had lusts.

By continuing to think on the Word, the Lord Jesus had hidden the Word in His own heart. The Word of God hidden in the human heart strengthens it against sin (See Psalm 119:11). Jesus' prayer and fasting strengthened Him to successfully abort the lusts in His thoughts while the lusts were at the thought stage. Through extended time of prayer He released the power of God's Word, which He had previously read and kept in His heart. It was this power that the Lord Jesus used to take the lust captive. He did this by fixing His thoughts on God's Word in His heart. It is the Word that you have read, confessed and prayed upon that you use to quench every fiery dart of the wicked one.

Once taken captive the lust could not progress to the conception phase in Jesus' heart therefore Jesus did not sin. He pleased the Father. Fasting and prayer help us in this way. Without the lust conceiving, satan had no foothold.

The resistance that we experience in prayer is not up some physical mountain, shrine, temple or physical location on the earth. The resistance is mounted through the thoughts that we do not take captive.

These thoughts are the arrows that the enemy directs at our hearts. The intention is to introduce wrong thoughts into our hearts, which will redirect the power of God in our lives. If we permit it, these thoughts will waste the power that we had previously supplied in the place of prayer.

We are to let the Word of God become our thoughts before, during and after we have prayed. This way peace keeps our heart secure while the power of God is working for our good to produce change.

2

FOUNDATIONS

Let my prayer be set forth before thee as incense; and the lifting up of my hands as the evening sacrifice.
Psalm 141:2

God showed the Psalmist that He receives our prayer as incense. The real meaning of the Old Testament was that it served as a parable of Christ (See Lk. 24:44). Therefore we know that this reference to incense describes Christ who is the fragrance of all real prayer. Our prayers as an incense describes Christ as the foundation of intimate communion with the Father God. Our prayer life is not based on how much we sweat, scream or repeat ourselves even. The foundation of prayer is Christ. He is that sweet fragrance.

When we pray from a consciousness of what Christ has accomplished, it is the purest perfume in the nostrils of God.

When in the middle of the mess of life, with our backs against the wall, rather than bawling and squalling, we go against the flesh and the world by lifting up our hands to God – that is sweet perfume.

God definitely hears prayer but it is clear that when prayer becomes praise and thanksgiving God also smells our prayer.

We are to be in continual communion with the Father, so that all that we do in words, thoughts and deeds are done in the name of Jesus. We maintain continual communion with our Father God not only through our words but also through thoughts energized by God's Word as well as our actions that correspond to our faith.

Concerning prayer, the Lord Jesus, through the Holy Spirit instructed the Apostle Paul to tell the Ephesians;

Use every kind of prayer and entreaty, and at every opportunity pray in the Spirit. Be on the alert about it; devote yourselves constantly to prayer for all God's people.
Ephesians 6:18 (GOODSPEED)

We are to be so established in Christ that we are skillful in praying different kinds of prayers. The Lord Jesus told us to love our enemies, to bless them and curse not (See Mt. 5:44). There are prayers that a Christian should not pray. If your prayer curses people by robbing them of opportunity, realization of potential and physical life you do not know what spirit you are of (See Lk. 9:55). There is no sweet fragrance of Christ in such prayers.

We are mindful of the fact that the best prayer to pray in a given situation is not based on formula or rules but the one that the Holy Spirit prompts us to pray. He will prompt you!

We are to stay full of God's Word and train ourselves to perceive the anointing to pray when the Spirit gives it. When we do not perceive this anointing to pray, we pray by our understanding of

God's mighty Word.

Writing to the Corinthian church that were no strangers to the manifestations of the Spirit, Paul said, "Now concerning spirituals I would not have you ignorant" (1 Cor. 12:1). In other words, a fellow can be exposed to lots of spiritual manifestations and still be ignorant about them! The same can be said of prayer.

The church is to learn to pray different kinds of prayers.

We hinder our effectiveness in prayer by assuming that one type of prayer fits all situations. Paul wants us to differentiate between the different types of prayer because different situations call for different types of prayer. As we gain understanding from the Word, we get better at cooperating with the Spirit as He prompts us to pray. Not understanding the different rules that govern different type of prayer would be as ridiculous as complaining that the players in a basketball game are not taking a penalty kick with their feet as the players would in a football match. Football and basketball are both ball games but they are worlds apart in organisation, team structure, rules and the way the games are played.

We remember that Paul was writing a letter to a church. No one writes letters in verses. Those verses were put in our bibles to aid easy reference. We lose nothing by removing the verses but retaining the words. If we read Ephesians 6:17,18 without paying any attention to punctuation or verse numbering, it would read like this: And take the helmet of salvation and the sword of **the Spirit which is the word of God Praying always** with all prayer and supplication in the Spirit and watching thereunto with all perseverance and supplication for all saints.

If we read it this way, it says that the sword of the spirit is the Word of God praying. We are expected to pray the Word.

Prayers like games come in variety. Like we showed earlier, anyone would be hopelessly confused taking the rules of basketball into a football game! Trying to use concepts of prayer of faith while praying for others needs to be handled skilfully. While We have authority over some spirits like demonic spirits we never have any over human spirits. When praying for others, we want to influence their wills not dominate them, which would be witchcraft. If people's wills and choices are involved you need to supplicate (or intercede).

Some concepts that work in prayer of consecration like "if it be thy will" will take you out of faith and bring you into unbelief when used in the prayer of faith.

When praying the prayer of faith for yourself, don't see how long you can be, but how short.

Give the Word first place

Writing to the Ephesians concerning the helmet of salvation, Paul said, "And take the helmet of salvation, and the sword of the Spirit, which is the word of God: PRAYING always with all prayer ......" (Eph. 6:17,18a). What he said about the helmet of salvation is true about every piece of the armor of God. The reason why we take on the whole armor of God is so that we can pray effectively. Every single piece of armor prepares us for prayer. Interestingly every single piece of armor refers to God's Word.

You will get more answers to prayer praying for yourself than you would running around going from convention to convention looking for someone of repute to pray for you. He does not say you are to get others to put on the armor for you.

We put on the armor knowing our privileges and rights as sons in the Father's family, knowing that we are satan's masters now and that we can enforce the victory of Jesus in our own lives. We are the heavenly aristocracy in Christ.

God confirms His Word

Then said the LORD unto me, Thou hast well seen: for I will hasten my word to perform it.
Jeremiah 1:12

God said that **He watches over His word to bring it to pass**. God does not watch over your prayers per se. He watches over His Word. If you pray His Word, then He'll watch over His Word within your prayer to bring it to pass.

Prayers can be hindered

Likewise, ye husbands, dwell with them according to knowledge, giving honour unto the wife, as unto the weaker vessel, and as being heirs together of the grace of life; that your prayers be not hindered.
1 Peter 3:7

Take note of that expression, "that your prayers be not hindered".

Though prayer is a divine exchange between God's Spirit and the human spirit where we send words and thoughts towards God who also injects His Word and His thoughts into our thoughts, prayers can be hindered.

The greatest hindrance to answered prayer is a **lack of**

knowledge of God's Word. Wherever we lack understanding of God's Word, unbelief and worry crowd into the heart. Anxiety, unbelief and worry plant themselves in the human heart to redirect the power of God in our lives. Unbelief and lack of knowledge will fight your faith by hindering your results.

We get more efficient in using our faith as we gain understanding of God's Word.

When God's Word is known the next greatest hindrance is **not acting** on God's Word as if it was true.

Another giant hindrance to prayer is refusal **to act** on the Word. You can be praying but yet not trusting God who is the greater one within you. When you fight your own battles you hinder God from bringing His own fight. You must pray and **act** like your prayer is working. People who know their prayer is answered boldly move on from prayer to laughter. Learn to laugh some more.

Born Righteous in Christ

Confess to one another therefore your faults (your slips, your false steps, your offenses, your sins) and pray [also] for one another, that you may be healed and restored [to a spiritual tone of mind and heart]. The earnest (heartfelt, continued) prayer of a righteous man makes tremendous power available [dynamic in its working].
James 5:16 (AMPLIFIED)

This is not teaching us to improve our morals in order to get God to answer our prayers. God does not pay you back with answered prayers because of your good morals. There is nothing in the whole universe that cripples a Christian like a lack of knowledge concerning the fact that we are as righteous as God and how His righteousness is the trigger for us to reign as kings in life.

For with the heart man believeth unto righteousness; and with the mouth confession is made unto salvation.
Romans 10:10

The New Birth is **"believing unto righteousness"**. We did not improve unto righteousness. We believed and we actually became recreated righteous. Righteousness is our spiritual DNA in Christ Jesus. God does not **make** unrighteous folks. He made us by birthing us in the New Birth. We are like Him in our recreated spirits.

For he hath made him to be sin for us, who knew no sin; that we might be made the righteousness of God in him.
2 Corinthians 5:21

You are born righteous in Christ.

Ours is a two-fold righteousness. Not only are we born righteous in Christ, Christ Jesus is made Righteousness to the believer. This righteousness is a gift. Since Jesus cannot become more righteous, the believer cannot grow in righteousness. We do not become less or more righteous. We however learn to be governed more and more by it and become skillful in using it.

Pray because you know that you are righteous. The prayer of a righteous person supplies tremendous power.

Dear friends, if our consciences do not condemn us, we approach God with confidence
1 John 3:21 (GOODSPEED)

Condemnation robs us of confidence towards God. Therefore

condemnation hinders faith from producing maximum results in our heart.

David was given the revelation of righteousness when he described the blessedness of the man against whom the Lord will not impute sin (See Psalm 32:2, Rom. 4:8). He said the Lord would not impute sin!

Redemption is God taking all that you were and blotting it out - good and bad! God does not recall your past simply because what you are now in Christ is not what you used to be before in the first Adam. The man in Christ has no past. You have no past. Understanding the realities of redemption gives you the ammunition with which you fight off condemnation, which is one of the hindrances to your faith. It rescues you from thinking, "because I was wrong yesterday, God won't give me so and so today". We remember that our morals did not qualify us, Jesus did. What a wonderful thing it is to be delivered from pride – pride thinks, "God answers me because I have never been wrong". Humility knows better. God answers me because he is an answering God. He can be nothing other than good. This causes us to bow in awe.

Sort out your thinking

But let him ask in faith, nothing wavering. For he that wavereth is like a wave of the sea driven with the wind and tossed. For let not that man think that he shall receive any thing of the Lord. A double minded man is unstable in all his ways.
James 1:6-8

Use God's Word to sort out your thinking concerning prayer - be specific, don't just pray in order to be praying. Some people are not specific in prayer; they are like tourists in a supermarket aimlessly pushing their trolley all day through the supermarket floor without picking anything from the shelves. They admire all that is on display but leave at the end of the day with aching legs, hungry stomachs and empty bags.

You release your faith first and then manifestation comes later. Pray God's Word and keep meditating on the Word so as to keep the Word in your heart. This means you see yourself with the answer. **Then learn the praise cure. Stay in Praise** by acting like God is not a liar.

Prayer is based on Words

And he said unto them, When ye pray, say, Our Father which art in heaven, Hallowed be thy name. Thy kingdom come. Thy will be done, as in heaven, so in earth.
Luke 11:2

God has created a voice-activated world for man. God Himself creates with His words. Prayer works because it is based on this bigger principle of spoken words.

You can speak without praying but you cannot pray without speaking. You cannot pray by thinking alone, you pray by saying. Yet we understand that our thoughts are involved in praying after we have done the speaking aspect of praying (See Phil. 4:8).

Let my prayer be set forth before thee as incense; and the lifting up of my hands as the evening sacrifice. 3Set a watch, O LORD, before my mouth; keep the door of my lips.
Psalm 141:2

The spiritual principle presented here is that our praying and our saying go hand in hand. Concerning his prayers he asked that a watch be set over the door of his lips. This implies that the mouth is a door into the heart. The reason why he wanted a watch set over his mouth after he has prayed is because people of prayer understand that their words release the power that their prayers make available. In addition the words that we speak out of our mouth can invalidate our prayers. **Saying** can cancel out **praying**. It is as we learn to use our words like spiritual machines that we discover that prayer is not magical.

For with the heart man believeth unto righteousness; and with the mouth confession is made unto salvation.
Romans 10:10

Your confession is your faith speaking. It was with your mouth that you made the confession unto salvation. Your faith keeps pace with your confession. This is because what you say is what you believe. You shall have what you say. You say it and then faith rises up to the peak of what you have said.

It does not matter if you have asked for wisdom on a matter, if afterwards you then say, "I don't know what to do", your words will prevent wisdom from bubbling forth. Learn to say "I have wisdom from God for this situation", and then act like you have that wisdom.

God has said in His Word, "I will never leave you nor forsake you" (See Heb. 13:5). Believe that. Act like God is with you. When you say, "Oh God be with me. Don't leave me", you are praying and acting like God is a liar. It is true that there will be times when you don't feel that God is with you, feelings are what they are, they will come and they will pass away. In those times hold fast to your confession by saying what God has said in His Word. Faith will create realities. It will bring feelings. If you say it, you will have what you say and that will bring feelings.

Inasmuch, then, as we have a great High Priest, Jesus, the Son of God, who has passed through the heavens, let us hold fast our confession of faith.

Hebrews 4:14 (MONTGOMERY)

You are to form the habit of speaking in agreement with God and then holding fast to that confession no matter what. If you do not learn to hold fast to your confession you will forfeit many victories that are already yours in Christ and which you already received in prayer.

But the word is very nigh unto thee, in thy mouth, and in thy heart, that thou mayest do it.

Deuteronomy 30:14

When we continually speak God's Words out of our mouth we release divine power on the earth. These words also form thoughts in our mind. As we think on these word-thoughts we focus and direct the power into our hearts. This focused power works within our hearts to enable our actions.

Our thoughts will channel our words into our hearts to produce actions. Said differently, we will do what we have prayed as we allow our thoughts focus the divine power released through our praying.

Increasing your spiritual sensitivity

It was as Peter was praying that he heard the Lord Jesus speak to him in a vision (See Acts 10:8-17). It was also as Cornelius was praying that the angel spoke to him to send for Peter (See Acts 10:2-3). This shows that the real benefit of praying is that it is a way of prioritizing our spirit senses over our physical senses. Real prayer awakens us to the spirit realm and helps us become more sensitive to God's Spirit.

Labouring in prayer

Epaphras who is also fruit of your ministry salutes you. What a diligent worker of Christ he is, always laboring on your behalf with great intensity in his prayers. His desire for you is to stand strong in the full accomplishment of Christ and to be fully persuaded in God's purpose for your lives.
Colossians 4:12 (MIRROR)

Paul commended Epaphras for labouring fervently for the saints at Colosse. Epaphras has great zeal for those he prayed for. Epaphras was the one that brought the gospel to Colosse. There are some prayers that you cannot finish in two minutes. Epaphras' ministry of prayer followed his ministry of the Word to the saints at Colosse. Paul also ministered the Word to the saints at Colosse. As a five-fold Ministry gift, Paul's ministry of the Word was to perfect the saints at Colosse. Epaphras gave himself to prayer more readily than the other saints or Ministry gifts in Colosse and God used him marvellously as a ministry of helps to the saints. We could all benefit from the helps that is supplied through persevering prayer.

Greek scholars tell us that the root word translated 'labouring' is the word from which we get our English word "agony". It indicates a wrestling or contention. We should pray with intense desire and deep-seated hunger within until the burden lifts and we have a note of victory.

A merry heart doeth good like a medicine: but a broken spirit drieth the bones.
Proverbs 17:22

We must not underestimate the energy that flows into our bodies when our emotions are intact. When we are praying about a crisis situation involving our relatives, it is good to take a break from observing their issue, which stares us in the face day and night. This is so that we do not get weary in our soul. When the soul is weary the body gets tired more easily. When the body is tired it is harder for the spirit's dominion to be expressed.

The use of His Name

Concerning praying in His name the Lord Jesus told the Disciples, Hitherto have ye asked nothing in my name: ask, and ye shall receive, that your joy may be full.
John 16:24

The Lord Jesus meant that up till that time His own disciples had not said any prayer in His name. Interestingly by this time He had already taught these disciples what some call **the Lord's Prayer**. Jesus meant that what we call **the Lord's Prayer** was not prayed in His name! Jesus taught a **model** of prayer to His disciples that they were to pray until that dispensation closed up. That prayer was accurate for the period that it was designed for. Today we learn from its model and not its exact wording. For example we don't expect God to forgive us as we have forgiven others (See Mt. 6:12). This is the nature of forgiveness under the Law. It was conditional forgiveness. However in Christ Jesus we have better things – We forgive others because we are already forgiven in Christ (See Eph. 4:32). What we call **the Lord's Prayer** is Jesus teaching His disciples a way to pray in the interval between His earthly ministry and His resurrection.

The Lord Jesus first gave to His disciples the power and authority to cast out devils and heal diseases. They carried this out in His name. This was an extension of His prophetic ministry. He had given them a limited power of attorney. Then in John 14, He takes them much deeper into this when He tells them something wonderful, "if you ask anything in my name, I will do it". That was not prayer. He was promising the disciples that a greater influence of power would be available through His name. They had His Word for it before He went to the cross. The Holy Spirit was given to supply the vital side and teach them the use of what Jesus had given them legally.

Don't empower the thief

Some people do not know that Jesus has carried all sicknesses and diseases. Some of these people believe that they are suffering for God's glory through their sickness. When people hear their testimony of suffering they become Christians. Some other people see that and pray, "if it be thy will that through sickness I glorify you, your will be done".

Peter told Cornelius that all the sickness that Jesus healed in His ministry was due to satanic oppression (Acts 10:38). Therefore, praying to glorify God through sickness is a way to open the door for satan to wreak havoc in the body. Anything done in ignorance, including prayer plays into satan's hands. This is because satan rules through darkness. Inaccurate praying empowers satan.

Fasting

As they ministered to the Lord, and fasted,
Acts 13:2

Under the Law the Jews had to fast on special days like the Day of Atonement. The Church is not instructed in the bible about how frequently or for how long we should fast. Fasting is obviously one of the ingredients that can help our prayer life. In the bible, fasting is connected with and is an aid to meditation, prayer and praise. Biblical fasting cannot stand alone. Fasting is giving ourselves over to feasting on God's Word, listening for His voice and praying extensively. When we try to make fasting stand alone it is glorified hunger strike.

Paul mentioned (but did not teach on) fasting (See 2 Cor. 11:27).

We approach the subject of fasting mindful that not once after His resurrection did the Lord Jesus instruct any of the New Testament writers in any of their epistles to instruct, teach or urge the believer to fast. That is a staggering fact when you consider that every single epistle contains instruction about prayer but not a single one instructed the church to fast! This does not do away with fasting but shows that it is up to the believer to determine by listening to the Lord those situations where fasting will help drive spiritual growth within the believer's life.

Fasting combined with prayer weakens the grip of unbelief on our heart (See Mt. 17:21). As we fast and pray our heart comes into unity because our soul submits more to our spirit. This causes more grace to flow from our spirit into our soul.

Since fasting is not taught in any of the Epistles we must be careful not to substitute it for depending on Christ in which case fasting becomes a dead work. This is so easy to do. The challenge is how to walk such that fasting does not replace dependence on Christ. We fast in faith on the basis of our completeness in Christ Jesus.

3

PRAYER OF THANKSGIVING

The prayer of thanksgiving is a supernatural communion between man on the earth and God in the spirit dimension. In thanksgiving we use our words, thoughts and actions to transfer gratitude from our hearts to the Father God for what He has already accomplished in Christ Jesus and its various effects in our lives today.

Continue in prayer, and watch in the same with thanksgiving;
Colossians 4:2

When we pray, God immediately releases the answer in spiritual form into our spirits. It is our responsibility and privilege to transform the answer into physical form via corresponding actions. One of those corresponding actions is the practice of continual thanksgiving.

Watching in prayer

Watching in prayer is the other part of the two-way communication system where you are looking out for directions from God to your spirit in the place of prayer; otherwise prayer is a lecture and not a dialogue. Thanksgiving in prayer is like the referee that ensures that the rules of dialogue are upheld. Prayer is primarily communion with the Father in words and thoughts and not vocalised murmuring or complaining.

Scope of Thanksgiving

We are to pray the prayer of thanksgiving for ourselves. When we pray the prayer of thanksgiving it speeds up the rate at which the peace of God moves into our heart from our recreated spirit. (Phil. 4:6). The peace of God delivers us from worry and gets us more God-conscious.

We are also to pray the prayer of thanksgiving for others just as Paul prayed for the saints at Ephesus (Eph. 1:16). Thanksgiving prevents us from complaining about saints. You are able to walk peaceably towards those for whom you give thanks.

We are to pray the prayer of thanksgiving for all men, especially those in authority (1 Tim. 2:1). This helps us live in peace towards all men.

God smells praise

By him therefore let us offer the sacrifice of praise to God continually, that
is, the fruit of our lips giving thanks to his name.
Hebrews 13:15

Giving thanks to His name means staying thankful for what He has already accomplished in redemption. We are affirming that Jesus dud it all. He qualifies us as worthy to receive the favour of God.

The fruit of our lips is equivalent to offering the calves of our lips (Hos. 14:2). This means that the sacrifice of praise fulfils the various calf offerings of the Old Testament. The sacrifice of our lips means that the offerings flow out to God through our mouths from our spirits. The burning of these calves releases a sweet smell. Therefore, thanksgiving flowing from our lips is the sweetest of fragrances to God.

As a New Testament priest offering the sacrifice of praise, God finds it praiseworthy when you burn off a little more of your dependency on the flesh. The death symbolised in such a fat offering is the death of dependency on the flesh.

The soul abdicates the throne for the spirit in the new creation and we are enforcing it every time we lift up our hands to the Father through thanksgiving. The lifting up of our hands in thanksgiving causes another stone to hit the Goliath of unbelief. Thanksgiving is incense. Our praise is His perfume.

God hears prayer but He smells thanksgiving and praise.

God is a singing spirit

The Lord your God is in the midst of you, a Mighty One, a Savior [Who saves]! He will rejoice over you with joy; He will rest [in silent satisfaction] and in His love He will be silent and make no mention [of past sins, or even recall them]; He will exult over you with singing.
Zephaniah 3:17 (AMPLIFIED)

When we say that God rejoices over us, we are saying that God is silent concerning and makes no mention of past sins. He does not recall them. When we rejoice in God it should be because we are silent over past sins also. We remember them no more. We remember Jesus.

Paul made an interesting statement while giving his guidance on the administration of utterance gifts in the church. The Holy Spirit revealed that when we give thanks in tongues we are giving thanks well (1 Cor. 14:17). Does He mean that it is possible to give thanks and it is not given well? If language means anything that must be the case.

Thanksgiving is at its peak when we give it in other tongues.

You see, singing of and by itself is not necessarily praise even if it is done within a church service with thousands of Christians gathered in solemn or festive assembly. If our songs are telling God not to remember what He has already assured us He would not remember, we are not thanking or praising God. If the wordings and slant of our songs hold God responsible for satan's deeds, we have not thanked God. That would be bearing false witness against His name.

Thanksgiving and singing go hand in hand because both God and man are singing spirits. If you stay thankful enough you will sing. God Himself rejoices over you with singing.

The sacrifice of our lips means that our confession in praise should be same as what God would say. The prayer of thanksgiving is like a prayer of agreement between you and God. You are moving to God's tune in intimacy.

I will not, I will not, I will not in any degree leave you!

Let your character or moral disposition be free from love of money [including greed, avarice, lust, and craving for earthly possessions] and be satisfied with your present [circumstances and with what you have]; for He [God] Himself has said, I will not in any way fail you nor give you up nor leave you without support. [I will] not, [I will] not, [I will] not in any degree leave you helpless nor forsake nor let [you] down (relax My hold on you)! [Assuredly not!]
Hebrews 13:5 (AMPLIFIED)

The Amplified version has God repeating Himself three times – I will not, I will not, I will not in any degree leave you! Once is enough from God but He said it thrice for our benefit.

All Believers are a holy priesthood. We offer up spiritual sacrifices acceptable to God through Jesus Christ (1 Pet. 2:5). If Jesus cannot offer the calves coming out of our mouth to God, then such do not qualify as praise. It is unacceptable. Jesus is both the altar and the sacrifice. We don't offer up or confess our experiences, pains, troubles or history to Him as thanksgiving. The content of our thanksgiving is Christ and what He has done.

Some of what we call thanksgiving and praise today makes for excellent melody but they unconsciously make God out to be a liar. Thanksgiving is meant to magnify God and not insult Him. Rather than sing, "I'm lost without you", we should remember that the one we are singing to cannot lie and He has already said that **He will not relax His grip on us;** therefore we are not without Him. Act like that is true by thanking He who cannot lie, the Father of glory, the mighty God, even He who has the last so for He has said He will not relax His grip on us in His Word.

All that we offer as the sacrifice of our lips, we do by Him.

The Old Testament says that God inhabits the praise of His people (Ps. 22:3). That describes His manifest presence. Those people were spiritually dead, therefore God could not inhabit them. They were not the temple of God. They had God visit them in the praise flowing from their heart. Their praise was the best thing that He could inhabit.

Today we are not waiting for the visitation of God. We are His lively stones, His temples. We are the visitation of God to our world. Our reality is that we are God's habitation (Eph. 2:22). Today God inhabits more than praise He inhabits you! That is what He has always wanted. As we give thanks His indwelling presence becomes manifest. It establishes a geography for the reign of God to flow through us like a Tsunami.

Faith overflows as we give thanks

Just like the roots of a tree draw your sustenance and strength from Him. Now you are displayed like a building rising up out of its foundation in His full stature, firm in your faith posture, standing tall in His shoes. The language of gratitude that overflows from your lips reflects the exact impression of what you were taught.
Colossians 2:7 (MIRROR)

The KJV says, "abounding therein with thanksgiving". This means that we abound in faith with thanksgiving. Thanksgiving is a way we complete our faith. If the walk of faith does not lead to thanksgiving, faith is incomplete. Thanksgiving is a way to make your faith continue to flow out of your heart. The resources in our spirit, including faith, flow out into our heart as we stay full of praise.

We unconsciously define thanksgiving in ways that make it look like living by sight instead of living by faith. In that sense, some limit their praise to gratitude shown for what God did for them recently. By that they mean that thanksgiving is our response to God when our situations turn around. Actually, real thanksgiving is part of the lifestyle of faith. It does not just concern itself with what the eyes see and the hands have handled. New Testament thanksgiving is strongest when you have no manifestation to point to and when things have not changed in the natural.

During the interval between the release of faith and the manifestation patience kicks in. This is when thanksgiving is needed the most. Instead of waiting for the manifestation to show up at which time we'll then praise God for what He has done, we praise Him continually for what He says is already done in His Word. When you know that the title deed is yours in Christ your heart sings. Waiting until your physical senses can see the answer before you give thanks is glorified unbelief. It is the Thomas kind of faith, the type that must see and feel before it awakens to God's faithfulness.

The prayer of thanksgiving magnifies God for translating us out of lack, darkness, anxiety and worry and translating us into abundance, light and peace in Christ. We voice out our consciousness of completeness in Christ. We let Him know that He has already met all our needs before we ever knew that we had one. The effect of that on us is that it rescues our soul from conforming to fear.

Do not forget His benefits

The Psalmist said,
> *Bless the LORD, O my soul, and forget not all his benefits.*
> *Psalm 103:2*

The mind of Christ is not forgetful therefore the saint should not forget God's benefits. Thanksgiving is a good way to school your soul into trusting God because of what He has already accomplished. The things that we are to thank God for have already occurred. They are not in our future, they are in our past.

As saints, we have conversations with our heart concerning the primacy of praise. Praise does not just happen. The unrenewed mind only breaks into spontaneous praise when the stars are in alignment, whereas the spirit trains the soul in conscious and deliberate thanksgiving. Faith agrees that God has already done it even if the senses do not yet see it. If we have to wait to see it before it leads to thanksgiving we are living by the senses.

We occupy the room of sons

Enter into his gates with thanksgiving, and into his courts with praise: be thankful unto him, and bless his name.
Psalm 100:4

Learn to read the Psalms with Jesus-tinted glasses. Jesus changes everything – especially how we read our Bibles!

The Old Testament saints were under the rule of spiritual death. They were outside God's court looking in at God who was in the Holy of Holies. The Holy of Holies was not their dwelling place. In fact their best was to send in a priest who entered in once a year by proxy and only for a few moments.

Thankfully that is not the case with the Christian. We are not in the outer court and a thick curtain is preventing us from God's presence. We are in the Holy of Holies and the Holy of Holies is in us (Heb. 9:24). The recreated spirit is God's Holy of Holies on the earth today. No, our spirit, the real us, is not trying to enter in. Jesus has taken us in. Jesus is our thanksgiving. When He entered to sit at God's right hand, we entered and sat down too. We are inside with God as members of the body of Christ. We are as much embodiments of God's presence as the Lord Jesus is. We entered His courts when we received eternal life. The songs that we sing out of our mouth do not cause us to enter His courts with thanksgiving today. Praise God! Jesus is our thanksgiving and He has taken us in once and for all.

In the New Testament since we are already seated with Christ, we are not attempting to enter into God's presence. We are identified with Christ at the Father's right hand. You see, we are the greater temple. We are what Solomon tried to build with the gold of this world but we are built without hands. We are the workmanship of God in Christ so we show forth the praises of Him who has called us out of darkness, depression and gloom into marvellous light. Thanksgiving is the gate that we use to increase our awareness of God's presence. We are ever in His presence. As we stay in thankful we break down the barriers in our soul that prevent us from acknowledging the presence and power of the living Christ. Glory to God!

Thanksgiving aids God-consciousness

Thanksgiving brings the manifest presence of God.

And when they had laid many stripes upon them, they cast them into prison, charging the jailor to keep them safely: Who, having received such a charge, thrust them into the inner prison, and made their feet fast in the stocks. And at midnight Paul and Silas prayed, and sang praises unto God: and the prisoners heard them. And suddenly there was a great earthquake, so that the foundations of the prison were shaken: and

*immediately all the doors were opened, and every one's bands were loosed.
And the keeper of the prison awaking out of his sleep, and seeing the
prison doors open, he drew out his sword, and would have killed himself,
supposing that the prisoners had been fled. But Paul cried with a loud
voice, saying, Do thyself no harm: for we are all here.*
Acts 16:23-28

Paul and Silas lifted their voice in thanksgiving and praise to
God. We know that this was not quiet thanksgiving because the
bible tells us that the prisoners heard them. There is a place for
loud thanksgiving. It is not so much because you want people to
hear you but because you are raining down fire upon the flesh
and unbelief. You are shouting down that loud noise inside the
head that tells you that it is over and you have lost. Thanksgiving
should replace prayer and become the highest expression of
prayer itself.

God rejoices over us with singing and we should rejoice with
him with thanksgiving and laughter too. Paul and Silas were
obviously not thanking God because of something they could
get out of it. They were thanking God because He was the focus
of their lives. This was proved when thanksgiving triggered a
local earthquake that broke their chains. The typical person who
is using thanksgiving only as a tool for deliverance quickly runs
out of that prison accepting it as supernatural deliverance in
response to praise. Paul and Silas kept right on praising the Lord!
The prayer of thanksgiving adjusts your awareness of God
until He becomes magnified in your world. These guys were
not praying the prayer of thanksgiving in order for God to do
something. It is always right to pray the prayer of thanksgiving
to God in the name of Jesus.

When we voice our thanksgiving to God, His peace in our
hearts amplifies His power planted within our hearts. God has
the opportunity to use the productive capacity of our heart to

produce freedom in our experience!

The opposite of this is in the admonition of the Apostle Paul,

> *Neither let us tempt Christ, as some of them also tempted, and were*
> *destroyed of serpents. 10 Neither murmur ye, as some of them also*
> *murmured, and were destroyed of the destroyer.*
> *1 Corinthians 10: 9-10*

When we do not stay our thoughts on gratitude, we stop peace from flowing from our spirit to our heart. The absence of peace in the heart allows the cares of this life and anxiety take our thoughts captive. When this happens we permit the planting of the cares of life into our hearts, which then produces the fruit of murmuring and complaints on our lips.

When we voice complaints the thief use our complaints to hijack the whole process and uses the productive capacity of our heart to multiply calamity!

As we grow in the grace of God it empowers us to let the fruit of our lips give thanks unto His name which is His nature and His character as seen in Christ. Pray the prayer of thanksgiving before, during and after any other prayer that you pray.

4

PRAYER OF COMMITMENT

In order to appreciate the reason for this prayer you need to examine some things that Jesus said about the drug called worry.

Here is what Jesus said,

Therefore I say unto you, Take no thought for your life, what ye shall eat, or what ye shall drink; nor yet for your body, what ye shall put on. Is not the life more than meat, and the body than raiment? Behold the fowls of the air: for they sow not, neither do they reap, nor gather into barns; yet your heavenly Father feedeth them. Are ye not much better than they? Which of you by taking thought can add one cubit unto his stature? And why take ye thought for raiment? Consider the lilies of the field, how they grow; they toil not, neither do they spin: And yet I say unto you, That even Solomon in all his glory was not arrayed like one of these. Wherefore, if God so clothe the grass of the field, which to day is, and to morrow is cast into the oven, shall he not much more clothe you, O ye of little faith? Therefore take no thought, saying, What shall we eat? or, What shall we

drink? or, Wherewithal shall we be clothed?
Matthew 6:25-31

Worry is filling our thoughts and meditation with the problem until our heart is filled with the problem itself. Worry makes the problem the treasure within your heart! Then your heart, which does not discriminate at all, makes the problem bigger by multiplying it. Through the abuse of the power of your heart, worry and anxiety steal the consciousness of Christ, who is the answer, from your thought life. Worry focuses on everything but the answer.

Thanksgiving is using our words, thoughts and actions to transfer gratitude from our hearts to the Father God. Worry is using our words, thoughts and actions to transfer complaints and murmurings from our hearts. Thanksgiving ascribes greatness to God while worry ascribes greatness to the problem and by extension satan. This makes worry a kind of worship service in reverse. Worry is really worship. Worry is demon worship camouflaged in socially acceptable garment. People "understand" if you are worried! Actually they shouldn't.

Any right-thinking Christians should distance themselves from idolatry. They should correctly agree that a Christian should not be found dancing to demonic drum beats in the deep forest. The same Christians do not understand that worry is exactly that!

We must walk free of this devil-taught habit of worry.

Worry is really a form of hypnosis where demons are practicing psychiatry. I find that when I say it that way it finally gets through to some people!

We are to let God's Word be our adviser. It is the best psychiatric treatment in the universe. Thankfully the Word of God, acting as our true psychiatrist, reminds us that God has already delivered us from all the power of darkness. He has translated us to the kingdom of sons. Sons don't worry.

Worry is a sin

It startled me the first time it dawned on me that the Lord Jesus did not give the prominence to any other sin that He gave to the sin of worry. Yet the church will accommodate, celebrate and promote a man who worries but come down hard on the man who smokes.

I am not for worrying or smoking because both are hallucinating drugs that are contrary to God's nature within my reborn spirit.

Now, smoking might not take you to hell but it'll sure make you smell like you've been there! While Jesus said nothing specifically about smoking, He did emphatically say we should not worry.

Jesus wants us to understand that worry is a sin.

In order to understand walking in sanctification, you must realize that God has already translated you out from under the power of any deadly habit including the habit of worry for that matter.

I am grateful to the Lord Jesus that He has personally delivered me from all the power of the enemy (Col. 1:13). That includes the habit of worry.

I have never smoked and never will. I keep saying it to plant the deliverance of Jesus deep into my heart so that my heart can keep manifesting more of that freedom that is my inheritance in Christ. That's the way of faith. Hypothetically if I were forced to make a choice between smoking and worrying I would take smoking over worrying (now that is shocking to some because to them man is all biology and chemistry therefore smoking is the greater evil. They still think worry is harmless).

Worry is the greatest addiction known to mankind. It is a product of fear. There are people who make healthy decisions on the food that they eat. They are unaware that the biggest meal known to man is the worry-diet. Most people eat food mixed with anxiety; therefore they cannot reap the full benefits of eating right. How about fasting worry?

The world of thoughts is one we should not take lightly.

That expression "take no thought" is enlightening. When Jesus used that expression "take no thought", He was referring to what we do with anxiety and worries in our thought life. Anxiety and frets are on offer but they are not from the Father, therefore we do not take them. Anxiety and worry do not just happen to us, we take them. They are not forced on us. We handle them with our thought life. Through our thoughts it gets lodged deep within our heart.

Thoughts are offered to us continuously by spirit beings both good and bad. As we let the peace of God dwell in our hearts we gain the power to cast down toxic thoughts.

Living worry-free

The fundamental reason why worry cannot dominate the believer is because Jesus has set us free by translating us out of the realm of worry into the kingdom of love as sons of the Father.

We take thoughts by giving them life through our words. Thoughts unspoken die unborn. Death and life are really in the power of the tongue (See Prov. 18:21). Our words will give life to thoughts because spoken words carry more authority and release infinitely more power than thoughts. God's thoughts within our hearts empower us to use our words to kill toxic thoughts.

We introduce God's thoughts into our hearts by hearing ourselves continually say the Word out of our mouth. This is how we replace toxic thoughts. We use words and thanksgiving to replace worry with peace. You can gauge which thoughts you have been taking by examining your words.

The new nature within the spirit of man is not compatible with worry. Learn to say out loud to yourself, "that thing called worry has no authority over me". We are free from worry. Do you believe that?

Be careful for nothing; but in everything by prayer and supplication with thanksgiving let your requests be made known unto God.
Philippians 4:6

Paul was teaching the saints at Philippi about getting results in prayer. He first instructed them to do something about **all** their anxiety. There is nothing worth worrying about.

Most people want to pray first and hold on to the cares but the Holy Ghost through Paul tells us to have zero tolerance towards worry first and then we are ready to pray. This is because when we hold on to worry it nullifies our prayer by resisting the power that we are releasing out of our mouths in prayer. When we take a thought into our hearts through anxiety, we are draining the flow of power out of our mouths. We are hindering the power of God from getting released for our good.

It would appear that the best preparation for a prayer meeting is to manage your thoughts and stay free of worry. The peace of God flowing from the spirit into the heart destroys worry. When we pray, we become more conscious of God's peace as it registers more in our hearts.

Peace comes as we focus our mind on God's Word (Isa. 26:3). We should have more worry-free meetings than we have prayer meetings. A life free from worry is a foundation for prayer. The old habit of worry can no longer dominate us. We are free. We are as free from worry as Jesus is free from worry because we share in the same new nature through the New Birth. It takes diligence in casting down thoughts and imaginations in order to demonstrate that freedom (See Prov. 4:23).

Now notice what the following portion of scriptures says,

> *Finally, brothers, whatever is true, whatever is worthy of reverence, whatever is just, whatever is pure, whatever is lovely, whatever is of good repute, if virtue is anything, if honor is anything, be always thinking about these.*
> *Philippians 4:8 (MONTGOMERY)*

We don't empty our minds in order to become spiritual. We fill it up with God's thoughts. After we have prayed, we are to protect our prayer "investment" by thinking along the lines of the desires that God's Word puts in our heart.

It is worthy of note that after instructing us on what to do leading up to praying, Paul teaches us to control our thought-life after prayer! Our thought life is more important than anything the devil is doing in or through others. Diligently using God's Word to manage your thoughts is a key ingredient of a successful life of prayer.

It would appear that our imagination and thoughts form the shape of what power would become in our lives. Prayer releases the power, after which our words releases the power, which we then direct, and focus with our thoughts.

Accept your freedom from worry

If you find that you are praying all you know to pray and doing all that you know to do and it does not appear to be yielding the results that you anticipate from the Word of God, check up on what you have been doing with worry. Worry hinders your inner man and destroys your vitality. Worry actually uses up the power that you are making available as you pray. This prevents us from releasing the critical mass of power needed to bring about the manifestation of the things believed in God's Word.

When it comes to worry, we must not try and get deliverance from something that Jesus has already delivered us from. We are to accept that we are free from worry and then act like it by tossing worry out of our life with the words of our mouth.

Casting the whole of your care [all your anxieties, all your worries, all your concerns, once and for all] on Him, for He cares for you affectionately and cares about you watchfully. Be well balanced (temperate, sober of mind), be vigilant and cautious at all times; for that enemy of yours, the devil, roams around like a lion roaring [in fierce hunger], seeking someone to seize upon and devour.
1 Peter 5:7, 8 (AMPLIFIED)

We are to commit our cares to the Lord once and for all.

It takes humility not to worry. That kind of humility exalts you over all of satan's scaremongering and fear tactics.

It is strange in deed when you find so many Christians who want to resist the devil but are happy to hold on to the habit of worry.

The idea is that satan feeds off worry. When you choose to be carefree (free from cares), you close satan's access to pressure you. In the final analysis, people become Olympic-grade worriers because they train at the gym of worry intensely every day. It takes practice.

We definitely have the ability to do something about worry because of the new nature within our spirit. This is why Peter tells us to cast it. We are to cast our cares upon the Lord. We are not told to inform Him to come take them out of our lives. There is a difference. He is our burden bearer. When we cast our cares by acting like worry has no grip on us, all those worries leave our lives. We no longer have them. We no longer have the cares. We are carefree. We became carefree over 2000 years ago. We are no longer taking thoughts. When we have casted our cares upon the Lord we don't go around discussing those cares with person after person for that is as good as taking them away from the Lord.

Planning is not the same thing as worrying. God wants us to plan but He does not want us to worry. Faith in God's Word causes us to go from worrying to laughing because our Father God has our back!

You see, we have been translated out of the family of worry, for satan's family is the family of worry. We have been translated into the family of rejoicing, thanksgiving and praise (Col. 1:13). We do not have a care in this world or the next one for that matter. We have redemption. We have a Father. We have society in God. God cares for us.

Peter uses a very strong term to describe what we are to do with our cares. We are to cast them. Casting is a conscious act that carries the idea of being decisive. You are letting the peace of God throw the care out of your thought life onto the Lord, who knows how to handle cares very well. You are divorcing your worries, so that it is no longer yours. Now it is up to God to sort out that care. This is not a temporary action. We cast with the intention of not picking it up again.

We are not told to cast our responsibility to think and plan to the Lord. The Lord will not do our thinking and planning for us. He will input into our planning as we take our place. We cast worries. Until you commit your cares to the Lord, you hinder your faith from bringing in the manifestation of God's provisions.

Learning to pray the prayer of commitment is one of the fundamental principles of the life of faith.

God keeps what we commit to Him

Reading the Amplified Bible translation of this verse, it adds the clause, "once and for all". The idea is that once we pray the prayer of commitment, we are to stay full of praise and meditate continually on things that are true, honest, just, pure, lovely and of a good report; otherwise, if there is no good report then don't report (Philippians 4:8). This means we do not plan to pick up those cares again in our thought life no matter what we are bombarded with. We rest in the Lord who is our burden bearer. Since He is bearing our burdens, we refuse to bear it.

For the which cause I also suffer these things: nevertheless I am not ashamed: for I know whom I have believed, and am persuaded that he is able to keep that which I have committed unto him against that day.
2 Timothy 1:12

Faith in God will cause us to know that God keeps the things that we commit to Him. God is not the one that commits and we are not the ones that keep. In order for God to keep it we must commit it to Him. We are to commit our cares, frets, worries and anxieties to Him. He never gives the burden back to us. We also never take it back. We are able to walk carefree (free of care). When people pass on cares to us through their words, we refuse to take those cares in our thoughts. Instead we pass them on to the Lord who is able to keep them. From that point onwards, we are to act like those cares have moved out of our lives forever.

Usually after praying the prayer of faith, we anticipate the manifestation of our answers. We let God's Word build within us the deliberate decision that we will not submit to worry. After we have prayed and the manifestation delays with the passage of time, satan transmits his lies to us as thoughts. He wants to convince us that faith has failed and the Word is not working. If we do not guard our hearts, we find that by thinking satan's thoughts we have received anxiety from satan. Some people then have a worry-vigil in unbelief. They find themselves getting anxious concerned that the result has not manifested yet. We can pray the prayer of commitment under those circumstances to cast our cares upon the Lord because we believe that His Word is working mightily within our heart and in our circumstance to bring us good.

We pray the prayer of commitment for ourselves. This is not a prayer that you can pray for someone else for you do not have the authority to commit another person's cares to the Lord. Don't forget that people can be interesting – they just might want to hold onto the addiction of worry! You give thanks concerning them and supplicate. You pray prayers that help them get a revelation of the peace of God within their own recreated spirits. You give them good Word materials to read without becoming unkind about it (We can be so intense we turn people off).

If after praying this prayer of commitment we fall into the

temptation to fret again, we repent and remind the devil that the habit of worry shall not lord it over us since the Son has translated us out of the domain of anxiety and we have cast those cares on the Lord. The best repentance is to rejoice in God and replace worry with laughter.

The prayer of commitment does not discuss our problems with the Lord. It is the prayer we pray to empty our heart of anxieties and worries that we commit unto the Lord.

5

PRAYER OF
CONSECRATION

*This was totally spontaneous, entirely their own idea, and caught us
completely off guard. What explains it was that they had first given
themselves unreservedly to God and to us.*
2 Corinthians 8:5 (THE MESSAGE)

The Macedonians had a strong revelation of God's grace that
caused them to give themselves willingly over to the Lord.
God does not override our wills for He does not want us to be
puppets. He wants us to yield our will to His will.

This is consecration flowing from a revelation of God's grace
and mercy.

As believers we aim to yield our own human will to that of God.

Jesus' example of consecration

Then cometh Jesus with them unto a place called Gethsemane, and saith unto the disciples, Sit ye here, while I go and pray yonder. And he took with him Peter and the two sons of Zebedee, and began to be sorrowful and very heavy. Then saith he unto them, My soul is exceeding sorrowful, even unto death: tarry ye here, and watch with me. And he went a little farther, and fell on his face, and prayed, saying, O my Father, if it be possible, let this cup pass from me: nevertheless not as I will, but as thou wilt. And he cometh unto the disciples, and findeth them asleep, and saith unto Peter, What, could ye not watch with me one hour? Watch and pray, that ye enter not into temptation: the spirit indeed is willing, but the flesh is weak. He went away again the second time, and prayed, saying, O my Father, if this cup may not pass away from me, except I drink it, thy will be done. And he came and found them asleep again: for their eyes were heavy. And he left them, and went away again, and prayed the third time, saying the same words. Then cometh he to his disciples, and saith unto them, Sleep on now, and take your rest: behold, the hour is at hand, and the Son of man is betrayed into the hands of sinners
Matthew 26:36 - 45

When we pray, we are supplying God's power (James 5:16). We are making God's power available and causing peace to be supplied into our heart from our spirit. This peace casts down any thoughts that are contrary to the will of God. It protects our hearts and mind (See Phil. 4:7). After we have prayed our thoughts then direct this power into our hearts primarily.

The Lord Jesus prayed a prayer having to do with subordinating His human will to the will of God. This is the prayer of consecration.

You pray the prayer of consecration for yourself.

The prayer of consecration supplies tremendous power into our hearts so that from our hearts we yield our will to God's will. As we think God's thoughts, our thoughts direct more and more of God's power into our hearts in order that our hearts empowers us to do the will of God on the earth. This focused power works within our hearts to enable our actions. The principle is that we will do what we have prayed as we allow our thoughts focus the divine power released through our praying the prayer of consecration. Our priorities after we have prayed the prayer of consecration then become a corresponding action to the prayer of consecration. Consecration releases action.

The major difference between this type of prayer and the prayer of faith is that while you cannot pray the prayer of faith until you are certain of God's will, you can pray the prayer of consecration when the will of God is not known.

This is the only kind of prayer where we use the phrase, "if it be thy will". The intention is to submit our will to God's will. This prayer does not channel God's power into your environment. It does not change things. It is designed to release tremendous power into the heart of the one praying it in order to affect the will of the one praying it.

You cannot pray this prayer for another person. Praying the prayer of consecration on behalf of someone else is nothing more than witchcraft and manipulation of their will. It is beyond the authority of the believer. We influence others as they watch our consecration to God.

Two-way communion

When we pray or speak God's Word we release power. We make tremendous power available. (Jam. 5:16)

After we pray, we set our souls to think on God's thoughts as a way to channel that power which we released through words in prayer. (Phil. 4:8)

Subsequently, the things that we think upon channel the power, which then ignites our actions. When we act correspondingly, it completes the cycle of prayer and brings God's will to pass on the earth. (Phil. 4:9)

Considering Philippians 4:6 – 8, we can define Prayer as two-way communion between God and man. Man replaces his worries with God's peace, frames God's Word in his thoughts and in his mouth. God gives answers to man as more thoughts and more actions for man to act out in order for man to harvest manifestation.

Thinkest thou that I cannot now pray to my Father, and he shall presently give me more than twelve legions of angels?
Matthew 26:53

Jesus' example of godly suffering

When that mob came to capture him, the Lord Jesus knew that He could have prayed a different type of prayer which would have assigned more than twelve legions of angels by faith in God's Word! That was His Bible right.

Jesus could have chosen not to lay down His life. He knew it. You recall that one angel took out 185,000 Assyrians in one night (Isaiah 37:36). Twelve thousand angels would have wiped out over 2 billion people on earth. In effect that would have been the end of the world.

Jesus' prayer of consecration had caused Him to willingly

forfeit the exercise of His rights to protection and supernatural deliverance. Even if He had not called for angelic assignment, He could have walked away from Gethsemane. The supernatural hedge of protection operating in the life of the Lord Jesus was so highly developed that when He declared His name to the mob that came to capture Him, everyone fell down to the ground (John 18:6). As an act of the surrender of His will, Jesus waited till He was captured. That's an example of Jesus' godly suffering. He had the chance to avoid being captured by that mob.

If you had your back against the wall and had no choice in a matter as a result of which you suffer, that cannot qualify as godly suffering.

When Jesus said, "nevertheless not as I will, but as thou wilt", He was using His Words to release power to enable Him yield His will to God.

You consecrate your will to God with words and then follow it up with actions that demonstrate a surrendered life. The consequence of praying the prayer of consecration was strength to do God's will. It also triggers angelic activity to strengthen us. These effects of the prayer of consecration are received at the end of the praying the prayer of consecration.

Strengthened to resist temptations

It was in the context of this prayer that Jesus told Peter:

Stay alert; be in prayer so you don't wander into temptation without even knowing you're in danger. There is a part of you that is eager, ready for anything in God. But there's another part that's as lazy as an old dog sleeping by the fire
Matthew 26:41 (THE MESSAGE)

Jesus was teaching Peter that praying the prayer of consecration strengthens us against temptations and distractions that come our way in the pursuit of God's plan. Jesus could not pray the prayer of consecration for Peter but Peter could have followed Jesus' example and prayed it for himself. His story would have been different when that girl questioned him about Jesus.

Consecration helps us discern timing

It was as Jesus prayed this prayer that He resolved not to exercise His right to pray the prayer of faith to receive supernatural deliverance. He knew it was not the time to pray such a prayer. The prayer of consecration deals with our conscience, motivation as well as our understanding of God's timing. Jesus received the strength to do God's will as a consequence of the prayer of consecration. This enabled Jesus to discern that it was not the time to walk away from the mob and much later that it was not the time to walk off the cross. He obtained strength to remain on the cross through his consecration to God. He did not take the thoughts from the mob that gathered at His crucifixion. If He had let those thoughts settle on His heart, it would have re-assigned the power He had made available in the place of prayer.

Notice that while praying the prayer of consecration in Gethsemane, Jesus went away again and prayed the third time, **saying the same words**. The fact that He used the same words thrice shows that you should pray the prayer of consecration more than once. Jesus prayed saying exactly the same thing in prayer thrice in one night! This shows that the prayer that Jesus used to surrender His will to do the Father's will is not the prayer of faith. You pray the prayer of faith once on a matter and afterwards you praise until manifestation comes.

The concept of consecration is contained in Romans 12.

I beseech you therefore, brethren, through the compassions of God, to present your bodies a living, holy sacrifice, unto God acceptable,—your rational divine service; 2 And be not configuring yourselves unto this age, but be transforming yourselves by the renewing of your mind, to the end ye may be proving what is the thing willed by God—the good and acceptable and perfect.
Romans 12:1-2 (ROTHERHAM)

Presenting our body deals with the realm of consecration. No one can present your body for you. We don't do this once. It is a life-long practice. Romans 12 shows that when we walk in consecration it is easier to renew our minds so that we can bring our souls to agree with the revelation of His will that God has placed within our spirits. This is how we come to prove God's will to such a degree that we become doers of God's will.

Once we pray the prayer of consecration and we become aware of God's will, we should then walk in the revealed will of God. Once we know the will of God, we should apply the concepts of faith to remove any hindrances, mountains standing in our way and receive provisions to fulfil God's will.

Faith working with consecration

Prayer of faith and prayer of consecration can work together. In that case, the prayer of consecration would precede the prayer of faith. Once you have prayed the prayer of consecration and you know God's will, you should use the principle of faith to move the mountains standing in your way preventing you from fulfilling the known will of God.

6

PRAYER OF FAITH

In starting, we must realise that

God is a spirit (John 4:24).

Man is also a spirit (1 Thess. 5:23).

God's answers are spiritual (Eph. 1:3).

Transforming answers into physical form

When we pray, God immediately supplies the answer in spiritual form into our spirits. He then expects us to use the principles of faith to transform the answer from spirit form into physical form. This would involve our corresponding actions. There is also spiritual resistance to manifestation of these answers mostly from satan and then from people who respond to him. This causes delays. This is where being skilful in the Word and knowing how to use your authority in Christ comes in. (See

Author's book "Manifesting answers to prayers").

According to James 5:16, when we pray, we are releasing God's power. We are making God's power available. We release power through our spoken words in order to bring about the manifestation of what God has said in His Word.

The source of faith

Faith comes by hearing God's Word; therefore God's Word is the source of faith (Rom. 10:17). Since faith comes by hearing God's Word, it must mean that if there is no Word for a thing, then there can be no Bible faith for it. You cannot exercise faith where there is no Word from God. Trying to exercise faith where there is no Word is really presumption and it could get you in trouble.

In God's Word, we find that God has not given us dominion over any other man. It is therefore impossible to exercise faith and authority over other people's spirit. Attempting to do so would be witchcraft and not faith.

Our heart, our mouth and our believing

Concerning the principle of faith, Jesus said the following:

For verily I say unto you, That whosoever shall say unto this mountain, Be thou removed, and be thou cast into the sea; and shall not doubt in his heart, but shall believe that those things which he saith shall come to pass; he shall have whatsoever he saith.
Mark 11:23

On a similar note concerning the prayer of faith, Jesus said the following:

Therefore I tell you, whatever you ask for in prayer, believe that you have received it, and it will be yours.
Mark 11:24 (NIV)

If we combine the thoughts in these two verses together, we see that the prayer of faith deals with our heart, our mouth and our believing. Until there is harmony between the heart, our mouth and what we believe, the prayer of faith cannot be prayed.

Receiving what is already fulfilled in Christ

The emphasis of the prayer of faith is not about making requests to God. When we pray the prayer of faith we are not making requests to God. The prayer of faith concerns itself predominantly with receiving because God has already provided for those things we believe to receive in Christ.

There are other types of prayer where there is an emphasis on making requests to God but those would not qualify as praying the prayer of faith. You pray the prayer of faith for God's promises, which the Word of God reveals to us are already fulfilled in Christ in the past. Salvation from spiritual death and health, are already sorted and fulfilled in Christ in the past. Healing and salvation are not things that God is about to provide. He has already done all that He would in providing Christ as Saviour, healing and health. We just need to learn how to receive.

While the redemption that we have in Christ is far reaching, there are other aspects of that redemption that are not yet fulfilled, though they are part of God's program for us. For example though the Bible speaks about the second coming of Christ and the glorified body, which are parts of the blessed hope; both are unfilled and are in the future. You cannot pray prayer of faith for that.

While ministering on the Day of Pentecost, Peter said that it was Christ exalted at the right hand of God that received from the Father the promise of the Holy Ghost, which He then shed forth in a way those gathered could see and hear (Acts 2:33). The Lord Jesus gave the Spirit on the Day of Pentecost. The disciples who gathered together before this event would have waited in hope since at that time that Day had not yet fully come. The fulfilment was in the future for that particular bunch. Therefore at that time whatever prayer the disciples prayed could not be the prayer of faith. They supplicated.

Once the Holy Spirit had been given, from Acts 2 onwards, we find that the disciples prayed differently. Men began to use the prayer of faith in receiving the initial filling with the Holy Spirit. Whenever we find the disciples praying in Acts, they did not pray that God should give the Holy Spirit, they prayed that the people they ministered to might receive (Acts 8:15). When provision has been made in Christ and the promise has been fulfilled, if we pray about those provisions we use the prayer of faith.

Changing things

For this cause, I say unto you — All things, whatsoever ye are praying for and asking, believe that ye have received, and they shall be yours.
Mark 11:24 (ROTHERHAM)

It is worthy of note that this prayer works best on things. You use it to change things and receive new outcomes from God through His Word.

Works best for you

The word "you" (or ye if you use the King James' version) occurs five times in that verse. This shows that the prayer of faith is not designed with other people's will in mind. It is a prayer primarily for you. The human will that comes into play is that of the one praying this prayer. There is nothing about this prayer that involves travailing, tears, groaning or strong crying. The prayer of faith is prayed after we have known God's will through his Word. Therefore, there is no "if it be thy will" about this prayer. You do not pray this prayer to obtain faith. Faith comes from hearing God's Word. You pray this prayer to release your faith so as to receive what you know God has already provided for you in Christ.

The intention when praying the prayer of faith is to find out how short it can be, not how long.

If we perceive a sensation, within our hearts, of someone falling through a set of stairs, the first thing some of us would do is assume it is about us personally, so we would by faith receive protection and safety in Jesus name. That's all well and good until we find out that afterwards the sensation has not left us. The Lord Jesus could very well be sharing someone's predicament with you. He would want you to persevere in prayer for those concerned until the danger is averted. The Lord Jesus in Heaven would be using the power that we supply through prayer to bring deliverance to those in danger. This is because the authority of this earth has been given to man on earth. Responding in love is the biggest ingredient in prayer. Since God is love and we are love children of the family of love, we will lend ourselves to the Lord in prayer for others. That would not be the prayer of faith. Not all our prayers have to be about ourselves. We are the marvelous body of Christ.

Remember that the Holy Spirit would not have instructed the church in Paul's letter to the Ephesians to pray with "all prayer", if he knew that the prayer of faith is the only type of prayer needed and that it would do the job in every situation.

You should learn to pray the prayer of faith. It will mostly be for you or for bona fide spiritual babies receiving through your faith. However, the more you pray for others you'll find that other types of prayers are needed.

The tenses of faith

Therefore I tell you, whatever you ask for in prayer, believe that you have received it, and it will be yours.
Mark 11:24 (NIV)

You will notice that there are three tenses involved. You are praying now. You received in the **past** and shall have in the future.

The heart and mouth must agree

The prayer of faith is heavily dependent on the heart because faith is dependent on the heart. The principle is that we speak out of our mouth what we believe is already provided in Christ. While doing this, we must not doubt with the heart but believe that we have received what we spoke out of our mouth in prayer. In other words, what goes on in your heart determines whether what you say in prayer will become manifest or not. The principle of faith is that the heart can invalidate or uphold the mouth. That principle means that the heart and mouth must agree on a matter in order to bring manifestation.

The Bible gives us a lot of detail concerning how faith receives from God (See author's book – "Manifesting Answers to Prayers"). We can see a lot of these at play if we pay close attention to how Abraham brought forth Isaac by faith. The Bible nowhere states that Abraham prayed the prayer of faith, but we can learn the principles of faith from his story since The prayer of faith is based on the principles of faith.

God used the first 24 years after Abram heard the promise of God to correct Abram's damaged vision. Then when Abram was ninety-nine years old, he was ready for God to teach him the value of confession. God taught Abraham about the confession of God's Word by changing his name from Abram to Abraham. Three months of daily intense fight of faith through hearing himself being called what God had already made him caused Abraham's body to be quickened, so he could get his wife pregnant (Rom. 4:19). Sarah's womb had been dead so that she had never been able to give birth to a child (Rom. 4:19).

God also taught Sarah the value of confession by changing her name. When Abraham and Sarah's faith acted in concert for three months after their names were changed, conception occurred inside Sarah. This couple then continued in the principles of believing what they had spoken out of their mouth for the next nine months until Isaac was born.

Isaac was born as a result of the heart and spoken words of Abraham and Sarah coming into agreement with God's promise. This settled into their hearts and their hearts rejuvenated their bodies until they became young again. They then got together in corresponding action and Isaac was conceived. The prayer of faith harmonises our visions, our believing and our words in prayer.

Concerning the heart-aspect of faith, we are to put God's Word in our mouths and use those words to frame the imagination of our hearts. Putting God's Word in your mouth will cause the imagination of your heart to be highly developed until it becomes like a spiritual machine that generates godly experiences. Use God's testimony of what is accomplished in Christ to frame your imagination.

Some prayer types work together

The prayer to receive forgiveness from God is the prayer of faith since forgiveness is already provided in Christ. On the other hand since this type of prayer would be heartfelt, the prayer to receive forgiveness also qualifies as the prayer of supplication. This hints at the fact that the different prayer types function like the gifts of the Spirit. They work together but we study them separately in order to understand them better so we can maximize their benefit.

Carrying others on your faith

You can carry your spouse on your faith if your spouse is a bona fide spiritual baby. You might help your spouse understand that he/she can receive from your faith. The effectiveness of that will reduces over time because God would not want your spouse to remain a spiritual baby. God wants spiritual babies to grow up.

Giving thanks always

Because you are identified in the Name of Jesus Christ, you can afford to always overflow in gratitude to the Father, (not for everything that happens to you but) in spite of everything that happens to you; you are not under circumstances but above circumstances because you are in Him!
Ephesians 5:20 (MIRROR)

The King James says we are to give thanks always. We pray the prayer of thanksgiving before, during and after praying the prayer of faith. The will of God is thanksgiving. Real Bible faith moves from prayer to praise. When we give thanks it causes our faith to abound (Col 2:7).

7

PRAYER OF SUPPLICATION

Some time ago at one of our prayer meetings, we had an open session where we discussed the different types of prayer. I discovered that not much was said about the prayer of supplication (nor was there much written about it).

The word "supplication" occurs about 68 times in my copy of the King James Bible. We ought to know what this prayer type is about.

Scope of Supplication

The prayer of supplication and the prayer of thanksgiving have the widest scope of all the types of prayer available to the church.

We are to supplicate for other saints. (Eph. 6:18)

We should supplicate for ourselves. (Philippians 4:6)

We supplicate for all men especially those in authority whether they are believers or not. (1 Tim. 2:1)

We can even supplicate in the Spirit. (Eph. 6:18)

When James described effectual fervent prayer he was talking about supplication. Supplication is intense and heartfelt (James 5:16).

What is supplication?

David said, "Let my supplication come before thee: deliver me according to thy word" (Ps 119:170). We would not be wrong to say God delivers by His power. David says that God delivers according to His Word. His Word therefore is His power. We base our supplication on God's Word.

Praying always with all prayer and supplication in the Spirit, and watching thereunto with all perseverance and supplication for all saints;
Ephesians 6:18

What does Paul mean when he said we should supplicate? We know that this is a type of prayer, for he mentions it in the context of prayer.

He encourages us to supplicate again in Philippians.

Be careful for nothing; but in every thing by prayer and supplication with thanksgiving let your requests be made known unto God.
Philippians 4:6

Supplication is making requests to God. It is unlike the prayer of faith in that respect. If you do not understand the principles of faith and the prayer of faith, you would most likely supplicate when you should have prayed the prayer of faith. In the New Testament, you don't supplicate for salvation, health, financial increase or healing. Those are all received through faith because they are fulfilled already in Christ.

Through His redemption Christ has given us a solid foundation for making requests and receiving answers to our prayers. As our hearts awaken to these rights we are able to act on our spiritual initiative to ask for the fulfilment of these things.

Jesus supplicated

Who in the days of his flesh, when he had offered up prayers and supplications with strong crying and tears unto him that was able to save him from death, and was heard in that he feared;
Hebrews 5:7

While He was on earth the Lord Jesus evidently prayed the prayer of supplication a lot. It is therefore important to understand the difference between the prayer of faith and the prayer of supplication. There are similarities as well as differences between the two.

Supplication in Acts 1

These all continued with one accord in prayer and supplication, with the women, and Mary the mother of Jesus, and with his brethren.
Acts 1:14

These disciples were waiting for the Lord Jesus to release the gift of the Holy Spirit into the earth for the first time. They were not passively waiting. They waited through praying the prayer of supplication. Though the Lord Jesus is a man, after His ascension to heaven, His influence over the affairs of the earth had reduced. The Lord Jesus could not give the Holy Spirit until Pentecost. He worked through the disciples on earth as they prayed continuously. They did not pray once then stop. This continuous prayer described during this period of waiting could not be the prayer of faith since you use faith to receive what is given by releasing faith from your heart. These saints were praying the prayer of supplication. This prayer was continuous. Supplication involves perseverance. We persist in these things because it is easy to become too conscious of the mental realm, our everyday life and to forget to pursue things to conclusion in the midst of all that.

We must be able to differentiate between a burden lifting because we switched off and we actually praying unto peace. Another thing to note is that a whole congregation can supplicate about the same thing at once. The prayer of supplication can be individual or communal. When supplication is done on the congregational level concerning the same thing, you are also describing united prayer.

Prayer in Acts 8

Now when the apostles which were at Jerusalem heard that Samaria had received the word of God, they sent unto them Peter and John: Who, when they were come down, prayed for them, that they might receive the Holy Ghost:
Acts 8:14-15

Take special note of how the disciples prayed in Acts 8. After Pentecost, since the Lord Jesus had already given the Holy Spirit, there was no use requesting Him to give that gift again. From that time onwards you never find the disciples praying the prayer of supplication about it again because the promise to give the Holy Spirit had been fulfilled at Pentecost. They prayed and laid hands in relation to people getting the initial filling of the Spirit, but the prayer was so that those they ministered to could receive by releasing faith from their heart.

Congregational Supplication in Acts 4

And when they heard that, they lifted up their voice to God with one accord, and said, Lord, thou art God, which hast made heaven, and earth, and the sea, and all that in them is: Who by the mouth of thy servant David hast said, Why did the heathen rage, and the people imagine vain things? The kings of the earth stood up, and the rulers were gathered together against the Lord, and against his Christ. For of a truth against thy holy child Jesus, whom thou hast anointed, both Herod, and Pontius Pilate, with the Gentiles, and the people of Israel, were gathered together, For to do whatsoever thy hand and thy counsel determined before to be done. And now, Lord, behold their threatenings: and grant unto thy servants, that with all boldness they may speak thy word, By stretching forth thine hand to heal; and that signs and wonders may be done by the name of thy holy child Jesus. And when they had prayed, the place was shaken where they were assembled together; and they were all filled with the Holy Ghost, and they spake the word of God with boldness.
Acts 4:24-31

This is an instance of a whole congregation praying the prayer of supplication together. They lifted up their voice to God. "With one accord" means that they were saying the same thing. It is likely that Luke got hold of a copy of the prayer that they prayed and he included it in the book of Acts. It would appear that the saints wrote down their supplication.

At first they magnified God in line with the Genesis account. They then directly quoted Psalm 2. They brought God's attention to the fact that people had ganged up to threaten them. They then made their request for boldness to speak the Word. This in turn would allow them to preach the Word to their adversaries who would then get saved.

In this prayer, they wanted God to supply boldness to speak the Word. The prayer of faith does not require God to supply anything. Their request was answered in the form of the filling with the Holy Ghost, which caused them to speak the Word with boldness. As they went out to minister the signs and wonders flowed.

The Pauline Prayers

A lot of Paul's prayers for others were prayers of supplication after he had prayed the prayer of thanksgiving for them.

For example when Paul told Timothy that he had without ceasing remembered Timothy in his prayers night and day, he was describing supplication (See 2 Tim. 1:3).

Notice that he prayed this type of prayer night and day! It was continuous and repeated.

Supplication is fervent, repeated, continuous, heartfelt and "without ceasing," type of prayer.

There were also other prayers whose contents are recorded for our benefits in Paul's epistles. Paul was not praying these prayers for himself but for the saints in various churches. These Pauline prayers fall into the category of prayers where other people's wills are involved.

In almost all the letters that Paul wrote to each church, he communicates doctrine and also shows them how he prays for those saints. Paul had prayed those prayers so often that he wrote it down for the saints, so that they knew what he had been praying for them. Writing it down caused all of them to see and hear the same thing, so they could come into one accord as they prayed it for themselves as an assembly. At the point where the saints start praying those exact prayers for themselves, the prayer becomes a big prayer of agreement between Paul and the whole assembly. If they prayed it prompted by the Spirit we could say it is a form of supplicating in the spirit. These prayer types are linked.

Following Paul's lead in his letters to the various churches, our prayer of supplication can be written down, spoken out and repeated word for word every time we pray them.

Supplicating to increase revelation and spiritual growth

As we examine the contents of those prayers of supplication that Paul prayed for the churches we can get a clue as to the repeated and "without ceasing" characteristic of these prayers.

While praying for the Ephesians Paul said the following:

I am sure you can appreciate how the news of your faith and love greatly inspires me. I am so happy for you; my thoughts and prayers are full of you. I desire that your knowledge of the Father will be undiluted, that you will draw directly from the source; that the God of our Lord Jesus Christ imparts the spirit of wisdom to you in the unveiling of His Master Plan (glory.) I pray that your thoughts will be flooded with light and revelation

knowledge; that you will clearly picture His intent in identifying you in Him so that you may know how precious you are to Him. The saints are His treasure and the glorious trophy of His portion! (We are God's assets and the measure of His wealth!)
Ephesians 1:15 – 18 (MIRROR)

He is making a request to God. The intention of this prayer of supplication is so that the born again one can be quick to grasp spiritual truths and realities. The reason is because the heart can be slow to understand. When this is the case it limits the reborn spirit from expressing its riches and hinders spiritual growth. The Holy Spirit was rolling upon Paul the infirmity of dullness of spiritual perception, which was hindering the Ephesians from growing up spiritually.

This was similar to the way he prayed for the Colossians.

Supplicating to combat spiritual ignorance

For this cause we also, since the day we heard it, do not cease to pray for you, and to desire that ye might be filled with the knowledge of his will in all wisdom and spiritual understanding;
Colossians 1:9

Everywhere you see Paul praying the prayer of supplication it is accompanied with intense desire.

The intention of this prayer of supplication is to combat spiritual ignorance in the heart of the born again one. Ignorance is not bliss. It robs the believer of dignity and honour. God wants us to have an exact knowledge of His will.

Repeating your supplication

Take note of the fact that Paul said "Cease not to give thanks for you, making mention of you in my prayers". He said to the Colossians, "do not cease to pray for you, and to desire". Whatever type of prayer this is, Paul repeated it often. He likely repeated it verbatim. This is why he could write out the exact words of his prayers. He prayed this prayer over a long period and repeated his desire in prayer often. Paul did not pray these prayers as the prayer of faith, which is prayed once and followed through with thanksgiving every time we remember the prayer.

We don't pray these Pauline prayers as prayer of faith. These Pauline prayers can be prayed many times a day and for however long we chose.

You don't use the concepts of the prayer of faith where you should be engaging the principles of supplication. The key difference is that if what you are praying about falls within the scope of things that are already fulfilled in Christ, you receive them through the prayer of faith. Don't forget this rule: for things already fulfilled in Christ Jesus, use the prayer of faith.

Supplication takes time

Cease not to give thanks for you, making mention of you in my prayers;
That the God of our Lord Jesus Christ, the Father of glory, may give
unto you the spirit of wisdom and revelation in the knowledge of him: The
eyes of your understanding being enlightened; that ye may know what is
the hope of his calling, and what the riches of the glory of his inheritance
in the saints,
Ephesians 1:16-18

The prayer for revelation takes time. They are prayers of supplications. The prayer for spiritual growth is also supplication. The prayer that we pray for those that minister the Word of God to us is the prayer of supplication. This is the prayer that Paul requested of the Ephesians (Eph. 6:21). Looking closely at the prayer that Apostle Paul told the Ephesians to pray for him, we see that the prayer for boldness to speak, as we ought to speak is a prayer of supplication also. We can pray such prayers for ourselves as well as those who minister to us.

Intense desire

Speaking of the Lord Jesus the writer of Hebrews says:

Who in the days of his flesh, when he had offered up prayers and supplications with strong crying and tears unto him that was able to save him from death, and was heard in that he feared;
Hebrews 5:7

The Lord Jesus offered up prayers and supplication with strong crying and tears unto God!

That term "strong crying and tears" implies that the Lord Jesus prayed the prayer of supplication at a depth that penetrated into His emotions. It stirred spiritual hunger within His soul deeply. The prayer of supplication adjusts the emotions.

We must remember that prophecy after prophecy already existed in God's Word concerning the things that Jesus was to fulfil. Jesus' life had been well documented in the Bible before His birth.

The Lord Jesus was not ignorant about these prophecies, for the Bible records in Matthew 26:24 that Jesus said, "The Son of man goeth as it is written of him:" Therefore, the Lord Jesus knew and believed these prophecies. Since Jesus knew and believed these prophecies and walked in God's will for His life, why supplicate at all and with strong crying and tears for that matter?

Jesus supplicated in order that those staggering unfulfilled prophecies of His life were not yet fulfilled. They were in His future. The prophecies concerning His death could not be fulfilled early in His ministry. It would be at the close of His earthly ministry.

When the various things that God spoke to us are not yet fulfilled, it is not enough to just know that He said them. We can supply supplication to bring about our growth and their fulfilment. It was because of these unfulfilled promises that Jesus prayed the prayer of supplication several times. Supplication is not based on ignorance. The prayer of supplication is based on what you know in God's Word.

So, why did the Lord Jesus not simply believe and receive it settled once and for all time according to what He taught in Mark 11:24? The fulfilment required Jesus to grow. He was going to be at His peak in the hours leading up to His crucifixion. It was in Jesus' future. Those things **required His growth and His obedience**.

Now when all the people were baptized, it came to pass, that Jesus also being baptized, and praying, the heaven was opened, And the Holy Ghost descended in a bodily shape like a dove upon him, and a voice came from heaven, which said, Thou art my beloved Son; in thee I am well pleased.
Luke 3:21-22

Luke makes an interesting point in his account of the baptism of Jesus in the Jordan. He is the only Bible writer that records that while John was baptising Jesus, Jesus was praying. Both John and

Jesus knew that Jesus was going to be anointed and announced to Isrealat this event (John 1:33).

At the start of that "ceremony", Jesus was not yet anointed for public ministry. It was as Jesus prayed that the anointing came. The Spirit had not yet descended upon Him when He started praying. Jesus was praying the prayer of supplication, in order that the promise might be fulfilled. Again, the principle is that if that which you pray about is already fulfilled in Christ, you believe you receive through the prayer of faith. For things promised and unfulfilled, especially things that require you to grow spiritually, you pray the prayer of supplication.

Persevering in supplication

Praying always with all prayer and supplication in the Spirit, and watching thereunto with all perseverance and supplication for all saints;
Ephesians 6:18

Notice that perseverance and supplication go together. Supplication harmonises the heart by affecting the soul so that it can be a good servant to the spirit. That takes time. Supplication requires perseverance because it takes time and except we discipline ourselves to pursue after the things of the Spirit, it is easy to get distracted from completing our supplications. We persevere with the burden, leading or knowing that the Lord has given us until we pursue it to conclusion and the victory is obtained. There is no burden associated with the prayer of faith. You are receiving for yourself in the now because the Lord Jesus has already made it yours in the past.

We ought to take more time to supplicate for all the saints just as Epaphras laboured in prayer in order that the saints at Colossians would stand perfect in all the will of God. We see glimpses in the

Old Testament that the best judges are priests. These are priests who judge. A leader prioritises the delivery of the Word to the people of God above everything else and then perfects them further through continuous prayers for those very saints. The Word is foundational requirement for growth. Following that, prayer opens them up to God's Word that delivers transforming power into the heart of the hearer. We often rush to correct when we should have prayed first. The correct order should be teaching, prayer and then counselling. Saints who are taught God's Word then need to be prayed for especially by the one who is delivering the rebuke. You correct better when you first prayed for the one you want to correct or counsel. We are first priests before we function as "judges". Biblical counselling produces relief but does not come anywhere close to the lasting answers birthed through prayer and counselling.

Praying and Travail

My little children, of whom I travail in birth again until Christ be formed in you, I desire to be present with you now, and to change my voice; for I stand in doubt of you. Tell me, ye that desire to be under the law, do ye not hear the law?
Galatians 4:19

Paul had prayed for those Galatians to receive Christ at the beginning. His prayers for them served as a great help when he preached the Gospel to them. They became Christians by receiving the Gospel into their hearts. He was now travailing again for Christ to be formed in them. They desired to be ruled by the Law. They had the new nature but were willing to hold it in bondage to the Law. Legalism is more appealing to the flesh than the grace of God. Paul had caught on to the heart of God on the matter. He wanted them to walk free of the bondage of legalism. They were to embrace the grace of God.

Travail is supernatural sharing in the burdens that the other is under. Usually, you would not need to pray travailing prayers for a believer except of course that believer had abandoned the grace of God like the Galatians did. Such travail is like coming under the pressure that their soul is subjecting their spirit to. You do not pick up travail by working yourself up emotionally or by directly observing the people that you were praying for. The Lord Jesus is directly touched with the feeling of the infirmity of legalism that these Christians were subjecting themselves to. Through our communion with the Lord He is able to pour their travail into our heart for us to deal with in prayer.

Travail is a temporary suspension of your sense of peace within. It is as though peace were withdrawn from your heart. The peace is still within the spirit since it is yours in Christ. In travail you are being used to offload the weights that the precious people of God are carrying.

When we have discharged this enormous pressure by praying it off, peace returns to our heart and the ones we have prayed for experience victory over the crisis that had held them bound. In the case of these Galatians, they would become strong in God's grace. Paul's prayers for them could only bring about that desired effect because someone was already giving the Word which imparted the knowledge of God's grace.

We repeat the prayer of supplication until the manifestation comes. It is not the prayer of faith.

PRAYER OF SUPPLICATION

8

PRAYER OF
AGREEMENT

Amplification of Power

It was Moses, who said,

> *"one shall chase a thousand and two ten thousand"*
> Deut. 32:30

Given that one puts a thousand to flight, we would understand it if Moses had been inspired to say that two shall put two thousand to flight but that is not what he says.

He said two should put ten thousand to flight.

This is a strange ratio in deed for it is not simple arithmetic. Moses was referring to the concept of the amplification of the supply of spiritual power when two saints agree on a matter.

He means that the act of agreement amplifies, at least ten-fold, the effectiveness of the faith of each of the saints involved in this agreement. The parties involved are supplying power as they pray (Jam. 5:16) and the agreement is exponentially multiplying the power supplied by each.

What Moses was saying can be paraphrased as "Two saints can put ten thousand enemies to flight because when we agree together their god abandons them and flees in terror".

The power of agreement

This is the way Jesus said it,

Again, I tell you, if even two of you here on earth agree about what they shall pray for, it will be given them by my Father in heaven. For wherever two or three are gathered as my followers, I am there among them.
Matthew 18:19-20 (GOODSPEED)

P. C. Nelson, who was a foremost authority on the Greek New Testament, said that the force of the literal translation of Jesus' statement here is, "If you shall ask anything in my name and I don't have it, I will make it for you".

Jesus is one of the parties to every scriptural prayer of agreement.

While the Bible teaches the concept of agreement, we sometimes miss what the real intent of Matthew 18 is. It is not primarily about praying the prayer of agreement in order to get your personal needs met (God definitely meets our needs in Christ Jesus).

What the Lord Jesus had been discussing in Matthew 18 is how we maintain fellowship amongst the saints by forgiving one another. He is detailing the procedure by which the love of God gains a brother back into fellowship with God's Word and with the saints.

At the onset there are two saints - The saint who is the offender and the saint who the trespass was committed against.

He is telling the saint whom the trespass was committed against to be the big one who is restoration minded. Jesus wants this saint to be mature enough to **first privately** confront the offending saint.

If there is no progress, Jesus then teaches that the mature believer, who is restoration-minded, should find other mature believers who come into agreement with the Word and with each other concerning how to rebuke and restore the brother who has sinned. The idea is that we jointly administer restoration or rebuke in order to avoid one saint abusing another. These mature ones agree on the approach that best brings God glory and unifies the saints.

He refers to this as binding and loosing. This binding and loosing is designed to bring benefit to the offending brother who is in the wrong. We wont give up on him. We are loosing the work of God into the lives of those who have done wrong by showing them mercy and forgiving them. This is the same thing Jesus did when on the cross He said, "Father forgive them for they know not what they do".

The mature saint has chosen to loose the offender from their trespass that they committed against him. This mature one now treats the offender as forgiven. He now calls other mature saints to witnesses his love-choice.

These brethren can use prayer to express their agreement. This would then be the prayer of agreement. One person speaks the technicalities of what needs to happen and the other person agrees with it as stated. You release agreement through spoken words.

The rules for the prayer of faith apply to the prayer of agreement. Before you pray the prayer of faith or prayer of agreement, you must feed your heart on the Word until you have that inner knowing that you will receive. You don't repeat the prayer of agreement. Repeating the prayer invalidates the agreement.

There are prayers where we need to bring other believers' hearts and minds into agreement with the image that the Word has built in our heart. If you can get another Christian to agree with you, you release tremendous power through that agreement.

If any two on earth agree

Jesus said, "if any two on earth agree". Thus the conditions for this prayer are that the parties have to be on earth and they have to agree. A closer examination shows that there is a numeric limitation involved. Jesus said, "if any two agree" and later He also said, "for where two or three are gathered". Strictly speaking this would not be a prayer between four believers.

This prayer works for whatever two or three believers can agree on in His name. That means they are to agree on anything that Jesus can put His name to. There is a Word basis for it. Jesus is personally in our midst to bring that agreement to pass.

There is a big "if" involved here; by this Jesus implies that it is not as easy to get an agreement partner. The most important thing in the prayer of agreement is the agreement that the people release from their heart.

PRAYER OF AGREEMENT

The prayer of agreement is not the prayer prayed holding the hands of other believers. The holding of hands is purely symbolic; it is not the agreement itself. Some people make it look like the tighter the grip, the stronger the agreement but that is not the case. Quickly grabbing the hands of the nearest believer to you and believing that they have agreed with you in prayer is ridiculous at the very least.

It is impossible to agree on the unknown. Be specific when you pray the prayer of agreement. If you are not specific, you are not in agreement with the Word or with another Christian.

Agreeing with Jesus

Again I say unto you, That if two of you shall agree on earth as touching any thing that they shall ask, it shall be done for them of my Father which is in heaven.
Matthew 18:19

We do not read this specific passage in isolation therefore we recall that what Jesus is really discussing here are the procedural steps for the assembly when believers are in dispute and one of the brethren insists on being divisive. The starting point is not twitter or Facebook but private rebuke between those in dispute. If this fails it is not the end of the road, other mature ones are to be called in. Yet Jesus presses the issue that we do not live in a paradise where all brethren are quick to repent. There are those instances where you meet that troublesome brother who would not acknowledge his fault nor would he listen to any of the one or two more elders who get involved. It is because he completely disregards the Word that he disregards everyone involved.

The one or two elders are involved based on the principle that it is the mouth of two or three witnesses that establishes a matter.

103

The two or three in agreement are the brother who wants reconciliation together with the one or two elders who were the witnesses who have listened to both parties in dispute and are interested in bringing glory to God by mending the breach between brethren. (It is also possible that the people in agreement were the very ones that were previously in dispute but have now found peace to forgive one another).

The Lord is really saying that when these mature ones form a quorum and agree on a course of action for dealing with the matter, God Himself will support their agreement because they are doing all things in the name of the Lord Jesus. They are taking a course of action that the Lord Himself would have taken. Jesus would have gone after the sheep that was lost. He would extend forgiveness.

If we hold on to their trespass, we are unable to bind and loose.

We loose them by forgiving them the debt owed by their trespass. The ones in agreement are agreeing on what best brings glory to God in that situation. When these saints agree that they loose the mercy of God upon that brother because Jesus already died for his sins, the Lord Jesus Himself shows up to agree with them that the record against that troublesome brother is clean. Jesus is released to pursue that person with His love. Our agreement with (or against) the Word releases great power. Where power is not understood, its exercise can bring great harm.

Does it apply to any thing?

Let us consider the statement again,

Again I say unto you, That if two of you shall agree on earth as touching any thing that they shall ask, it shall be done for them of my Father which

is in heaven
Matthew 18:19

Someone might read that and come away with the conclusion
that the prayer of agreement applies to **anything**. They think
that they now have a scriptural way to bring any thing to pass in
any one's life through their prayer life. Is this a promise that any
prayer request will be granted once we go via the route of prayer
of agreement?

Applied to the concept of the prayer of agreement, if Jesus
wanted us to read this as applying to any thing, then any two
believers can use prayer as a cover for determining outcomes
in other people's lives whether or not those people consented.
Though Jesus said, "If two of you shall agree on earth **as
touching any thing** that they shall ask", the Lord Jesus was not
making a blanket statement.

When people exercise their choices, we cannot just override
their choice by what we believe to be good for them in prayer
using either the prayer of faith or prayer of agreement. Both
the prayer of faith and the prayer of agreement have an implied
scope that does not ordinarily extend into the lives of others.

In the same manner that the prayer of faith is about you releasing
faith in your own heart to receive what is provided by God in
redemption, the prayer of agreement carries its own implied
scope. When used within its scope the prayer of agreement is
useful for unleashing tremendous power.

The "any thing", is primarily any thing concerning the two or
three people praying the prayer of agreement. It has to concern
the people praying the prayer of agreement. In other words, in
the normal sense, we pray the prayer of agreement with people
and not for them. When it is a prayer for others, the prayer types

most suited are the prayer of supplication or intercession.

Sometimes, people pray pious-sounding prayers like "I hereby agree with my brother Jonah that sister Mary is his wife in Jesus name". That would be enlisting God to force sister Mary to marry brother Jonah! Thankfully, that is not the way it works. Such agreement is presumptuous since God has not given any man dominion over another human.

Without learning to first hear God through His Word, two people avoiding the Word while trying to get into agreement with each other will ultimately reinforce each other's opinions on an emotional level. This would most likely enforce strongholds. When you hear God through His Word within your heart and you voice out what you have heard you unleash the power of God. On a very basic level, though brother Jonah likes sister Mary, sister Mary might not like brother Jonah that way. She is not required to. There is no chapter and verse that says, "I give Mary to Jonah by perpetual decree".

Some other fellow chooses not to "claim" a particular sister but prays to God to lead him towards a particular body shape. He meticulously reads out the skin colour, statistics and physical proportions that he is after "in Jesus name". Though specific names have not been mentioned, that prayer proceeds from lust. According to James, asking in order to consume upon our lusts is invalid praying (James 4:3). His heart is after a trophy and not a spouse. What would the motive of such a person be?

It is perfectly right to agree that someone who is a good fit for you spiritually, emotionally and physically will be guided by God into your life and you into theirs. The trouble comes when you start claiming specific individuals.

With whom do we agree?

If you study the tower of Babel one fact stands out - The Bible does not promote agreeing with each other without first agreeing with God. Therefore the prayer of agreement is the prayer prayed by two or three people who already agree with God. They are getting their hearts to agree with one another in order to supply tremendous power to change situations in line with God's Word.

When Jesus says, "for where two or three are gathered together in my name", that gathering together is more of a leading together. The Lord is the one blending all these hearts together in a most powerful way. The prayer of agreement is best prayed by two or three people who have practiced how to listen to God together. Their hearts are knit together by hearing each other repeat what each has heard God say on a matter. It is this confidence that forms the basis of their agreement. When we feed on God's Word and listen to our hearts we will find that we are led towards certain people with whom we can pray the prayer of agreement.

You develop your ability to agree with people over time.

Finding one with whom you can agree is not such an easy thing; especially if the person does not have the same need. The Greek word for agree here means to make music with all instruments available, to play the same tune or to harmonize. The picture is that one Christian sounds out what is in his heart, something he is sure that he has scriptural foundations for in Christ and the others listen for a similar note in their own hearts. Wherever they find that they are sounding the same note that is where they have agreement. They might not agree on every thing but they are to major where their hearts can make music together.

This is a two-fold agreement. In the first instance, we are to agree with God's Word. The Word then empowers us to agree with one or two others with whom we pray the prayer of agreement. You are only ready to pray the prayer of agreement after you have spent time meditating on God's Word. You will also notice that the prayer of agreement works best with two believers and at most three. When it comes to the prayer of agreement, it is definitely not the case of the more the people in agreement the merrier.

The people praying the prayer of agreement might find it beneficial to jointly decide to write out their agreement together with scriptural references backing each statement. This way they come into close alignment regarding their desire and provide an anchor for their soul as they agree.

We can get newborn spiritual babies to receive from God through our faith as we pray the prayer of faith, or they can believe that our agreement with them will work.

We can get the principle of the power of agreement to work between any two believers who get into agreement. If however, I know to pray for you but you are not available to agree with me I cannot pray the prayer of faith or the prayer of agreement for you. It will have to be a supplication in the Spirit. That type of praying requires perseverance, it is heartfelt, earnest and continuous.

Making music

The Greek word translated as agree means to harmonise with every musical instrument at your disposal. This refers to harmony of your heart, your belief and your actions before praying the prayer and especially afterwards.

*Then came Peter to him, and said, Lord, how oft shall my brother sin
against me, and I forgive him? till seven times?*
Matthew 18:21

Harmony is of the heart. It does not only refer to making melody
with those you want to get along with or those with whom you
hope to pray the prayer of agreement.

You will notice that just after the Lord Jesus taught about the
power released through the prayer of agreement, the only
question Peter sought answers to had to do with frequency of
forgiveness. From the way that Jesus had presented it, Peter
understood that the presence of disharmony in the heart and
actions of the ones praying the prayer of agreement can undo
the power supplied through the prayer of agreement.

It is as we learn to walk in love that our spiritual awareness of
the presence of the Lord intensifies. The Lord Jesus is present
before, during and after we pray but it is as we agree with the
Word and with others that we free up ourselves to discern Him.
On the other hand, if we do not walk in love the disharmony in
our hearts blocks us from seeing the Lord and His provisions
This disharmony in our walk effectively cancels out any answers
we already obtained through the prayer of agreement prayed
from the same heart! This means that forgiving others removes
any hindrance to your prayers. We are really making music with
every instrument available.

9

UNITED PRAYER

In order to understand united prayer we need to appreciate some facts about the way God has built man.

And the Lord said, Behold, they are one people and they have [a] all one language; and this is only the beginning of what they will do, and now nothing they have imagined they can do will be impossible for them. Come, let Us go down and there confound (mix up, confuse) their language, that they may not understand one another's speech.
Genesis 11:6 - 7

Some Bible scholars tell us that the events at Babel happened less than 150 years after the flood of Noah.

God observed what was starting to happen at Babel. The trouble could not be that God did not want them to succeed at building a tower to heaven. We find that much later Canaan was described as, "the cities are great and walled up to heaven" (See Deut. 1:28). The term just means that the walls or the tower would be very tall. How tall this could be is purely down to architectural know how. That is not sinful. The challenge God faced was what to do with men with incredible intelligence, wicked hearts and whose imaginations were evil continually who were now banding together. Given the slant of their hearts, they would form a critical concentrated mass for evil, which would mean that there would be no restraint of wickedness. There would be exponential escalation of wickedness unleashed by humans on one another. Mankind could arrive at wiping itself out on earth without a redeemer.

In mercy God took decisive action.

God was not being vindictive or punitive. He was preserving humanity.

This story hints at the concept that God has wired the human such that there is tremendous amplification of creativity and power, which is released when men speak the same things because they are pursuing the same purpose in the same time frame.

This power works irrespective of the morals involved. If it were only men with holy motives that could tap into and trigger that phenomenal power, there would have been no reason for God to act.

God acknowledged that these men had tapped into a reservoir of power that could be unleashed to devastating effect. The men were controlled by spiritual death, therefore, the power would have been used to kill and destroy. God had to intervene to prevent men from bringing harm to themselves.

Moses was referring to this concept of amplified power, when he said, "one shall chase a thousand and two ten thousand" (Deut. 32:30).

Avalanche of power

The church is the body of Christ. We give him legal expression on the earth.

Each member of the church possesses the life of God through the New Birth. Each member is also made a kingly priest unto God; therefore when we are led into unity, it is the uniting of a company of kings and priests unto God (Rev. 1:6).

Individually, as we operate in faith, out of each of us rivers are flowing from the life of God within us (John 7:38).

When we have a sufficient mass of these kingly believers led into unity around one purpose and all are speaking the same things as the Head of the church, it forms the equivalent of a spiritual tsunami flowing from our hearts. We become one mighty stream of volatile supernatural power. This corresponds to the prophecy that God gave Solomon, "The king's heart is in the hand of the Lord, as the rivers of water: he turneth it whithersoever he will" (Prov. 21:1). We like to use that scripture as a basis to pray for political rulers but spiritually speaking we are the aristocracy of God. We are the kings who have yielded our hearts into God's hands to direct. In effect our prayers supply tremendous power, which God is able to direct as we yield to Him. The water of this tsunami refers to divine ability flowing from the belly of the kings who possess the life of God. The Lord Jesus, as the prince of these kings, is able to use the authority supplied by His kings to good effect on the earth.

Triggering the corporate anointing

When the Church prays speaking the same words as the Lord

Jesus as they pursue His purpose, the corporate anointing is triggered. United prayer manifests the power of the corporate anointing as no other type of prayer can. In such an atmosphere, there is amplification of the words spoken by each person in unity who is pursuing the same purpose. The primary reason that satan encourages believers not to gather together with other believers is so as to prevent the release of amplified power. Unlearned believers look for every excuse known to man to avoid coming together with other saints. They think they are protesting against those believers whereas they are protesting against the exponential power they could have supplied for the Lord's use.

Keeping the unity of the spirit

We should labour to be of one mind with other believers so that we can form a community of power. Hence, we make every effort to keep the unity of the spirit in the bond of peace (Eph. 4:3).

All believers are one spirit with the Lord. God guaranteed that in the New Birth. This is not where our challenge lies. The challenge we face stems from the fact that not all believers pursue unity with other believers. Our hearts need to become knit together as we pursue love.

Believers who don't believe along the same lines tend to approach things from different viewpoints and these viewpoints birth different practices. Add to this the fact that Christians are people and some people just get along better with certain people than they do others. Therefore, some Christians get along better with certain Christians than they do others.

If we all learned stay sensitive to the Lord, we would find Him leading us into unity of heart around His plan.

God wants us to be of one mind.

A few believers whose heart and minds are united around a common purpose are more effective spiritually than thousands of believers who are not in unity though they are uniform and they are gathered under one roof.

Uniformity is not unity. Uniformity is fleshly and it draws power from us while draining us. Uniformity causes us to look to one another. Unity focuses us on the Lord and not on our differences. Unity causes us to directly cooperate with the Lord, which makes us cooperate indirectly with each other. Unity amplifies our collective power.

Agreement is in degrees

At critical times, the Lord Jesus did not take the biggest crowd with Him. He did not reason that the larger the crowd, the more beneficial spiritually.

On the night of His betrayal, Jesus took eleven disciples with Him to Gethsemane. Then of that lot, He went farther with three of His disciples who were to pray with Him (Mk 14:32-38).

On another occasion, He turned back everyone including His own disciples and took only Peter, James and John with him (Mk. 5:37). Without a doubt, Jesus gave Peter, James and John a lot of attention. This is because they were likely the weakest initially; therefore, they were the ones the most in need of attention among the disciples (See 1 Cor. 12:23). Peter, James and John required rapid growth for the work ahead.

On the other hand, Peter, James and John had run a business together, before Jesus called them to ministry (Lk. 5:10). These men had spent time in each other's company and had learnt how to get along with each other. It is likely they carried this over into doing ministry with Jesus. The level of power generated though their unity was more pronounced because the level of resistance arising from disharmony between them was low. The level of agreement among the twelve was not as highly developed as that amongst Peter, James and John. The flow of power was in degrees because the level of agreement was in degrees.

One accord

And when they heard that, they lifted up their voice to God with one accord, and said, Lord, thou art God, which hast made heaven, and earth, and the sea, and all that in them is:
Acts 4:24

Each believer has the indwelling anointing of the believer. The prayer of agreement, prayer of commitment, prayer of consecration and the prayer of faith draw heavily upon this anointing of the believer.

When believers come together in unity, the corporate anointing comes into play. This is a kind of prayer that draws heavily upon the corporate anointing. This type of prayer featured a lot in the book of Acts when the whole assembly of saints came together in prayer.

In united prayer, every believer present is praying saying the same words and galvanized by the same purpose, at the same time. If there is division and tension amongst these believers, their division cancels out and redirects the tremendous power released by such united prayers.

In a sense, when we pray united prayer, our united speaking is converting the corporate anointing to power that can be used to meet needs in that assembly or elsewhere.

Those who are praying the united prayer would usually be at the same location as is the case in the book of Acts.

The Lord Jesus attempted to pray the prayer of consecration as a form of united prayer by inviting His disciples along with Him to the place of prayer. That never materialised because while Jesus continued in prayer, the disciples all fell asleep.

United prayer in the spirit

There are instances where the Lord Jesus by the Holy Spirit transfers the same prayer to different Christians even if they are in different locations. If they all respond to this at the same time, that would qualify as a united prayer in the spirit, even if those praying are unaware that there are others being stirred to pray along with them to reap a mighty harvest for God on the earth. Such prayer would be prayed in tongues or by inspiration through prophecy.

A deluge of power

And they were all filled with the Holy Ghost, and began to speak with other tongues, as the Spirit gave them utterance. And there were dwelling at Jerusalem Jews, devout men, out of every nation under heaven. Now when this was noised abroad, the multitude came together, and were confounded, because that every man heard them speak in his own language. And they were all amazed and marvelled, saying one to another,

Behold, are not all these which speak Galileans? And how hear we every
man in our own tongue, wherein we were born? Parthians, and Medes,
and Elamites, and the dwellers in Mesopotamia, and in Judaea, and
Cappadocia, in Pontus, and Asia, Phrygia, and Pamphylia, in Egypt,
and in the parts of Libya about Cyrene, and strangers of Rome, Jews and
proselytes, Cretes and Arabians, we do hear them speak in our tongues the
wonderful works of God. And they were all amazed, and were in doubt,
saying one to another, What meaneth this?
Acts 2:4-12

Take note of the fact that men spoke in other tongues because
God gave them the utterance by His Spirit. On the day of
Pentecost, when the saints started speaking in tongues, the
utterance did not come from man but from God. The utterance
for tongues is always divine in origin. Each man was cooperating
with something that originated in God.

There was a spectacular operation of the Spirit that caused
the spectators present at street level to spectacularly receive
understanding of what was being said. More importantly, they all
said that they were hearing the same thing (Acts 2:8)! All those
people that were present were hearing the wonderful works of
God. The reason why they were hearing the same thing was
because those 120 disciples that were speaking in tongues were
yielding to the coordination of the Holy Spirit into saying the
same things in the spirit and it was for one purpose.

This makes the event of Pentecost a case of united speaking.
If we consider that one shall chase a thousand and two ten
thousand, it means for every additional Christian participating
in that united speaking, the power multiplied 10-fold. When you
consider that at least 120 new creation men spoke in tongues
saying the same thing by the inspiration of God at the same time,
exponential power would have been released at Pentecost. What
makes this powerful is that the Holy Ghost is the orchestrator.

The Holy Spirit was an invisible conductor orchestrating the release of power at Pentecost. He placed something in each man's spirit, which they then spoke out as one voice in the spirit. That was a reverse of the tower of Babel.

Revival is when men act on the Word

What happened to all that power released though the mouth of men who spoke in tongues at Pentecost? This was the deluge of sufficient power supplied though speaking men. This supplied power was what God used to bring about His plan on the earth. Those words became thoughts, which channelled the power into the hearts of the speakers. The hearts thus saturated with these thoughts generated supernatural actions by the saints in the early church. These became the acts of boldness that characterised the disciples.

It wasn't that God stirred out of slumber and decided to act on a whim. God was not the one that revived. The men spoke the same things under the inspiration of the Spirit and caused a spiritual avalanche to blow through the land. This is coming in our day by the Spirit of God as men awaken to walking intelligently with the Spirit of God.

In Acts 4, they did not ask the Lord to remove their enemies from the earth nor did they ask God to stop the persecution. We do not know if one of the believers was leading the prayer. When the disciples prayed the united prayer in the book of Acts, all of them prayed at once and since it says they all lifted their voices, it means that they all prayed out loud.

United prayer tends to be prayed out loud. This was similar to Paul and Silas lifting up their voices at the same time. It was not just in their heads. The other prisoners actually heard them (See

Acts 16:25). This kind of prayer is often accompanied by visible demonstrations of God's power. In Acts 16 there was a localised earthquake that broke the chains as a result of this united prayer of praise. In Acts 4 the very building shook under the surge of God's power, which they supplied through their unity. Their unity unleashed the corporate anointing.

A lot of the prayers in the book of Acts are united prayer. Sometimes it was a united prayer of supplication making requests to God to bring certain promises to pass (See Acts 1:14). At other times it was united prayer of praise.

We should pray this was more often as assemblies.

It would be foolish if a Christian decided to abandon his own Christ-given private prayer life because he wants to function by the avalanche of power generated through united prayer. United prayer was not designed as a substitute for personal prayer. In fact united prayer is a continuation of the personal prayer lives of those involved.

United prayer involves us praying with our own company. Our company are those whose souls are knit together as one with us on a corporate level. It is not round the world praying. They had a specific reason. It is not a case of the more the merrier. It is a function of the corporate anointing and the unity of heart that taps into it. United prayer basically reproduces the concepts of the Tower of babel under the influence of God's Word.

10

PRAYING IN THE SPIRIT

The Lord Jesus, through the Holy Spirit instructed the Apostle Paul to tell the saints at Ephesus;

Use every kind of prayer and entreaty, and at every opportunity pray in the Spirit. Be on the alert about it; devote yourselves constantly to prayer for all God's people.
Ephesians 6:18 (GOODSPEED)

Notice he said, "at every opportunity pray in the Spirit"

This must mean that we are presented with plenty opportunities in the course of any given day to pray in the Spirit. It is up to us whether we seize these opportunities or not. God is not the one who determines the frequency – we do!

We are to devote ourselves to this type of prayer.

Again, since this praying in the Spirit should be done at every opportunity, we should aim to understand what it is as well as how to give ourselves to it fully.

The new nature helps our infirmity

Likewise the Spirit also helpeth our infirmities: for we know not what we should pray for as we ought: but the Spirit itself maketh intercession for us with groanings which cannot be uttered.
Romans 8:26

Notice that the Holy Spirit **also** helpeth our infirmity.

The use of the word "also" would mean that the Spirit is helping the believer in the same manner as another help that is already present in the believer's life. The first help that human beings get which gives them the advantage in life is the new nature of the born again human spirit, and then the written Word.

The reason why the Holy Ghost is able to help us in our infirmity is because our spirits have already been recreated in Christ.

The Lord Jesus by His Spirit also helps

The Lord Jesus, through the Holy Ghost, helps us in prayer by giving us utterances, impressions, urges, leadings or burdens in prayer. We then pray these out through the ability of the Holy Spirit.

Neither the Lord Jesus nor the Holy Ghost can do our praying for us. The Holy Spirit is our helper, who comes along to take hold with us against infirmities by giving us the ability to pray.

Since the Word tells us that the Holy Spirit likewise helps us, then we are to rest in the fact that He always helps us. Though the Holy Spirit can be relied upon to supply this help we might not take advantage of it if we are too distracted to sense the Holy Spirit taking hold with us.

What are these infirmities?

Infirmities refer to limitations in our souls and bodies. A believer that knows the Word of God would walk in the light and the light of life will pour health out of his spirit into his body. If he finds sickness fastening itself to his body, he would remember that Christ has provided healing in redemption. This is why the believer will use faith in God's Word to destroy that sickness. There are however, believers who are ignorant about their rights and privileges and are in need of help to get sickness off their bodies. That is an infirmity.

The Lord Jesus does not abandon them and leave them to wallow in their infirmity. We can expect the Lord Jesus to share with us the feelings of that believer's infirmity (Heb. 4:15). This way He is communicating divine compassion into our heart.

The infirmity is never in the believer's spirit. The major infirmities that the believer contends with are of the soul that is not grounded in the revelation of what Christ says is true about that believer. Sometimes, we read the Word and are not quick to perceive its meaning or application. At other times, we are not quick to acknowledge truth. These conditions are infirmities too. God wants us filled with the knowledge of His will as revealed in His written Word and the 'knowings' that He gives to us.

The Word will help us with general guidance, whereas the inward 'knowings' take over on those specifics of life where the Word is quiet.

We are co laborers with God. We follow his promptings and obey His leadings.

Praying by prophecy

This is the way that the King James reads,

Praying always with all prayer and supplication in the Spirit, and watching thereunto with all perseverance and supplication for all saints;
Ephesians 6:18

If we were to suppress these words, "with all prayer and supplication", the sentence becomes clearer. It becomes, "Praying always in the Spirit". Paul is making a case for us to pray as much as we can in the Spirit. We pray in the Spirit in our understanding as well as in tongues.

As Christians, we should be able to pray in the Spirit in our understanding. When we pray in the Spirit with our understanding, it is as though we are praying by prophecy.

The Holy Spirit supplies utterance, which we then speak out in a language that we understand. These are not words we have premeditated in our minds. They come through our mouth but they did not originate from us. Praying by prophecy is the same inspiration by which the urge to prophesy comes to us. Praying in the Spirit in our understanding carries a higher anointing than just praying our understanding of God's Word on a matter. If we are not careful, we can "waste" that anointing by exerting ourselves too much in the physical. A fellow who senses this urge to pray could unconsciously use up all the energy in vigorous shaking of the head and various parts of the body. At the end of that exercise, the person is physically drained and in need of a cure for body aches as well as neck pain.

The witness of the Spirit

The Spirit itself is a co-witness with our spirits that we are children of God.
Romans 8:16 (SAWYER)

Notice that the Holy Spirit does not directly relate with our brains or emotions but with our human spirits. He bears witness with our recreated spirits. He will supply witness to our spirits. This witness will help us know things as we pray in the Spirit for our spirits are capable of supernatural knowledge and insight.

Expect to know things supernaturally. Release your faith for it because the Word tells us that the Spirit will bear co-witness with our human spirits. When we pray in the spirit in our understanding, it will often register on our spirits as an urge to pray. That urge can be described as a burden or a leading. When you sense an urge, leading or burden to pray, it is best to find the time to yield your authority to God through the words of your own mouth; for prayer works best when voiced out.

When the Holy Spirit gives you a prompting to pray, He gives it to you because He is aware that you are available to do something about it. The urge, leading or burden will change in intensity as you can separate yourself from the affairs of this life. If you are unable to completely set yourself aside to pursue praying out this urge, you'll just take a longer time to arrive at the answer. God understands.

Align your will and cooperate with God

What is it then? I will pray with the spirit, and I will pray with the understanding also: I will sing with the spirit, and I will sing with the understanding also.
1 Corinthians 14:15

There is a principle involved here. The will of man is required in order for man to properly express the things of his own spirit, or any other spirit good or bad for that matter.

If you sensed this urge in a setting where you had to continue to talk to others, then find a way to express your will, even if your mouth cannot voice out prayer audibly. In today's world, it is not always possible to excuse yourself from the call of professional duty. Let the conversation with God continue within your heart until the burden lifts. The key is to find a way to use your will to give expression to the spirit. At the very least, you can speak very quietly at intervals or speak on the inside of you in your heart. Your spirit can lay a grip on the prompting that the Spirit gave to you. This is hard to do if your mind has not become developed to allow the reborn spirit have the ascendancy. Continuing this conversation within your heart is better than procrastinating and pushing the praying until later.

The principle is that the Spirit takes hold with us. What if the Spirit does not take hold with you as you expected? Do you flow with the Spirit or talk the Spirit into flowing with you? You flow with the Spirit.

Praying in tongues

But ye, beloved, building up yourselves on your most holy faith, praying in the Holy Ghost,
Jude 1: 20

The Apostle Jude expressed praying in the Spirit as praying in the Holy Ghost. He said this type of praying builds us up on our most holy faith.

Faith comes from God's Word and not from tongues.

The New Testament has a lot to say about praying in the spirit by praying in tongues. For example, Paul wanted us to let us into the secret of where got his profound wisdom when he made the following startling statement,

Which things also we speak, not in the words which man's wisdom teacheth, but which the Holy Ghost teacheth; comparing spiritual things with spiritual.
1 Corinthians 2:13

The Holy Ghost as Paul's teacher first taught Paul through a language that He supplied to Paul. This language did not flow from man's brain. Whatever Paul was saying through that language was actually Holy Spirit-taught words. Through this Spirit-taught language, wisdom was communicated to him beyond what his biological senses of seeing and hearing ever conveyed. It was through the words of this language that Paul received new light and fresh insight beyond what he knew when he was a Pharisee bound under spiritual death. This Holy Spirit-supplied language is none other than the spiritual language that we know as other tongues.

The supernatural language of tongues is a means of inward

revelation by which the Holy Spirit as our teacher unfolds to us the mysteries of who God is, who Christ is within us and who we are in Him. Speaking and praying in tongues this way was the means through which the Holy Spirit edified Paul to know the wisdom that was previously hidden in God. Paul exercised himself extensively through this means of spiritual edification until he wrote out whole epistles that he was then teaching to the saints.

In the spirit

For he that speaketh in an unknown tongue speaketh not unto men, but unto God: for no man understandeth him; howbeit in the spirit he speaketh mysteries.
1 Corinthians 14:2

Paul says that the fellow who speaks "in the spirit" here is speaking in an unknown tongue. He clarifies this further when he says:

For if I pray in an unknown tongue, my spirit prays, but my mind is barren.
1 Corinthians 14:14 (MONTGOMERY)

He says that praying in an unknown tongues is prayer done by the human spirit. Therefore, when Paul instructed the church to "pray always in the spirit", he meant that the Holy Ghost expects us to pray a lot in unknown tongues. Praying in the Spirit by praying in tongues is not all that there is, but it will unfold to you what the next step is.

The Greek word that is translated "tongues" in our English New Testament is better translated as languages. Even today, if someone were to ask you about your mother tongue, you would know they are not referring to the organ of taste but to your native language. Thus, there is really nothing mystical about tongues if you think of it as a language; for that's what it is. It would therefore help you, whenever you come across that word "tongues" to have "language" at the back of your mind, so as to remove any confusion.

When "unknown" and tongues are used together, a good translation would italicize the word "unknown". This is because it was added in our English Bibles to amplify to the non-Greek speaker that the language that was spoken was not a learned one.

What is speaking in tongues?

For if I pray in an unknown tongue, my spirit prays, but my mind is barren.
1 Corinthians 14:14 (MONTGOMERY)

Speaking in tongues is a conversation between our recreated spirits and our Father God. The Holy Spirit places the utterance within the spirit mind. Speaking in tongues is yielding your physical tongue to your spiritual tongue, so you can speak spiritual utterances generated within your spirit by the Holy Ghost. The Holy Ghost generates this utterance within your spiritual mind, which resides within your natural mind. In anatomical terms, your human will moves your biological tongue to push out as audible sounds, the utterance that is in the spiritual mind. We refer to these sounds as speaking in tongues. When speaking in tongues, we are bypassing our soulish mind and its limitations.

The Lord Jesus never prayed this way. Jesus never prayed in tongues, while He was on earth. This is because prior to the cross, Jesus had no sin in His spirit. therefore His mind had never been darkened by a dead spirit (Eph. 4:17-18). His spirit was always alive with the life of God. He had light in His spirit. The nature of spiritual death within the human spirit darkens and distorts the human mind filling it with vanity and emptiness. Since Jesus had no unrenewed mind, He had no need to bypass His human mind. Therefore He had no need for tongues. We do.

Activating the teacher within

Which things also we speak, not in the words which man's wisdom teacheth, but which the Holy Ghost teacheth; comparing spiritual things with spiritual.
1 Corinthians 2:13

The Holy Ghost is the Teacher who trains our new nature in comparing spiritual things. There is a language that the Holy Ghost teaches. This supernatural language compares the deep things of God's life with the things of our new nature. This language is not from our brain cells, from our culture or natural reasoning but from the intelligence of God within the spiritual DNA of the new nature in Christ. Our spirit maintains correspondence with God's Spirit (Rom. 8:16).

The supernatural language communicated by the Holy Spirit causes us to know the mind of the spirit. You come to understand many things that you don't know how you know them but you 'know' that you know them. This is the spiritual mind at work. When we speak in tongues, we are exposing ourselves to revelation and insight from God. It is really up to us to use the language that the Holy Ghost generates within our spiritual minds to lift us above the infirmity of ignorance, until He separates us unto the perfect plan of God for each situation that we find ourselves in. He will most definitely show us the next step in life. When we speak in tongues, the Holy Spirit is teaching us. When we pray out in other tongues, which is the language the Holy Spirit teaches our spirits, the mysteries spoken out are not the traditions, limitations and infirmities of men. It is God teaching us spiritual things. The Holy Ghost as the Teacher of our new nature helps us by taking those mysteries that we have spoken out to build out a syllabus for training us. This is the training that equips the spiritual one to judge all things from the mind of Christ.

Build on the ancient landmarks

Remove not the ancient landmark that the fathers have set
Proverbs 22:2

The wisdom of God causes us to consider those fathers who have lived out a life of spiritual excellence. They are pillars sustained by the revelation of truth. We do not reinvent the wheel when there is spiritual heritage of a foundation of revelation to build on. We build on the foundation of revelation knowledge already communicated through the Apostles.

Someone might ask, why don't we just pray in tongues exclusively, knowing that it will bring us to the revelation of the same mysteries that are in the Word? Why would we, for example, meditate on the written Word also?

Praying in tongues diligently will bring to you the same mysteries that are in the Word for it is the same Holy Spirit that inspired those writers that actually supplies utterance to us as we speak in tongues. This was the way that the fathers who wrote the various Epistles got the revelation that we call the written Word. Those fathers got the revelation of the Word from the Holy Spirit as they spoke in tongues hour after hour over a period of time. Many of them wrote those letters towards the end of their lives after a lifetime of practice of spiritual excellence perfected through speaking in the spirit extensively. The journey from receiving a revelation from the Holy Spirit in a step-by-step manner until you can write it down would sometimes take a lifetime.

Even when all those apostolic fathers prayed out the understanding of the mystery, they did so while paying attention to the written Word at their disposal. They paid attention to the foundation of revelation laid by those who had gone before.

If you do not give attention to what is already revealed in God's written Word, you would be doing yourself a great dis-service using only one weapon when there is a whole armor in God's Word. Moreover the more you speak in tongues the more you'll be pointed to other spiritual disciplines like meditating on God's Word and confession.

Hypothetically if you could function by only praying in tongues, it would take you your whole lifetime of diligence in tongues before you get a segment of a fraction of what Paul wrote. Then you still need to get what the Holy Spirit already gave to Peter, James and John. You would be racing against time. Time itself would run out. On a practical note, it is highly likely that you have not developed yourself to that place of diligence yet.

Even after you get the revelation of the mystery and have it taught to you from within, you would still be led into committing it to writing in order to meditate and act on it later!

You build on the foundation that is already laid in the Epistles so that you don't try to re-invent the wheel. Those are the ancient landmarks that the Fathers have set.

Help comes as supernatural utterance

As a new creation, the Holy Ghost helps you primarily by transferring into your spiritual mind, the exact contents of the mind of the Lord. This is because the capacity of your spiritual mind is the same as that of the Lord Jesus. It is not through the brain but through this spiritual mind that we grasp the plans of God. Your spirit is more intelligent than your brain and will pick up facts that your brain cannot substantiate at the moment.

The born again man has the mind of Christ which causes his spiritual eyes and ears to see and hear the plans of God. Our human spirit searches the deep things of God. It is our born again spirit man that speaks in tongues (1 Cor. 14:14), as the indwelling Holy Spirit generates the language by giving the utterance (Acts 2:4), which we then speak. (See author's book: The secret behind the secret)

You can quietly whisper your words in tongues in the most rowdy of train stations. Those barely audible sounds are edifying. There is nothing wrong with lifting your voice when speaking in tongues. You should do so more often when you are alone and you are not disturbing anyone. Disturbing those who are sleeping because you are praying in the Spirit is distasteful.

When you pray in tongues, you are mostly building up a lot of power for later use. This is very much like a wise person building a solid gold reserve in the bank for use at a later date. There is no limit to how much power can be released into your life for later use as you pray in tongues. If you learn to do this often, it builds you up and readies you for any emergency request for funds (power) in your life.

Interpreting our prayers in tongues

Wherefore let him that speaketh in an unknown tongue pray that he may interpret.
1 Corinthians 14:13

The plain reading of that scripture is that speaking in tongues in your private life also includes interpreting your prayer tongue.

You have a Bible-right to interpret your own prayers that you pray out in tongues.

We hinder ourselves from benefiting greatly from the riches of praying in tongues by thinking that tongues and interpretation is purely for public use when all the saints are gathered. It is true that there is a public side to tongues and interpretation under certain circumstances but as we pay more attention to Paul's letter in 1 Corinthians 14, we will discover that the main use of tongues and interpretation is in the private life. It is the badge of the church age. Its riches belong to every individual believer.

When I interpret my own prayers that does not make me an interpreter. It would just mean that I was one who prays in the Spirit. The gift of interpretation of tongues on the other hand would interpret **all public** utterances spoken out when saints are gathered in fellowship. You would not interpret what some other person prayed in tongues because that is private and not public. It is between the speaker and God and not between the congregation and the speaker.

If we were to interpret the prayers in which we edify and build ourselves up, we would find out that they are prayers of worship and praise. They do not have to be interpreted.

After praying in tongues a while, as we begin to interpret our prayer, we would find that we are sorting out things about the future or getting instructions about the things we are to do.

When interpreting you own tongues, you might find it prudent to pray a few words in tongues and then pray the interpretation.

You do not need to be able to interpret someone else's prayer in tongues. To interpret messages when other saints are gathered involves a different level of anointing supplied through the gift of the Spirit called Interpretation of Tongues. When the gift of the interpretation of tongues is in operation, it is not designed to interpret private communion but public messages meant for the saints who are gathered. As the chief minister of edification in my own life, I should be able to interpret my prayers in tongues.

Why would we interpret our prayers? It is so that together with Paul we can say, "What is it then? I will pray with the spirit, and I will pray with the understanding also: I will sing with the spirit, and I will sing with the understanding also" (1 Cor. 14:15)

What does Paul mean by, "I will pray in the spirit and I will pray in my understanding also"?

He is describing how we go from "tongues" to "understanding". It means that in the same manner as you have prayed in tongues, you will keep along that same supernatural track by receiving more utterance in tongues, which will require interpreting. Too many times, we just leave things up to God hoping He will get things sorted, when in reality He wants us to cooperate more with Him, so that He can work through us to bring about the best outcome as we stay yielded to Him. This is especially true in prayer. We start out in supernatural prayer and then we enrich our understanding, especially as we sing in the spirit and interpret the utterance that the Holy Ghost gives us. This takes us further in the plan of God.

Interpretation of tongues a key spiritual asset

When you pray in the spirit, you pray until you know that you know. That's when you stop. If you do not sense this knowing, you'll find that singing in the spirit quiets you. You stay quiet until you know within you the next step to take. As you practice this more, you'll find that you will receive supernatural utterance flowing out of you in tongues for interpretation. As you interpret this, you get direction about what next to do in order to arrive at the place where you know that you know.

You either pray until peace overwhelms you or you get information from within about what you need to do, in order to get to the place of peace.

Groans

Likewise the Spirit also helpeth our infirmities: for we know not what we should pray for as we ought: but the Spirit itself maketh intercession for us with groanings which cannot be uttered.
Romans 8:26

Likewise means "in the same manner". It is in the same manner as the bondage and groaning in the whole of creation because of Adam's treason (See Rom. 8:22).

In the Letters of Paul we find another type of infirmity. He describes it as the heavy burdens carried by weak Christians.

Weak brethren carry a lot of infirmity. This is the infirmity of believing the wrong things. They cannot eat certain meats because the butcher is not a Christian and he might have sacrificed it to his idol. They cannot buy certain houses because they suspect that the last owner belonged to the illuminati. It is these types of things that Paul calls infirmities. Such weak Christians are unable to walk in the liberty that Christ has purchased. We are to be strong enough to lift the burdens enforced by their slant in believing (See Romans 15:1).

We see an example of this infirmity in the life of Peter. Though the Lord Jesus had said to Peter, "and ye shall be witnesses unto me both in Jerusalem, and in all Judaea, and in Samaria, and unto the uttermost part of the earth" (Acts 1:8), Peter's tradition would not let him accept that this included Gentiles. He still saw them as unclean. He saw them as dogs. His traditions hindered the Lord from getting the gospel to the Gentiles. Jesus put him into a trance and gave him three visions and even then Peter still doubted that Gentiles should hear the gospel (Acts 10:16, 17). That was a chronic infirmity. If you had been stirred up to pray for Peter at that point, you'll likely find that there is a lot of groaning. You might not know why but you should yield to the Spirit as He attempts to lift the burden off Peter's religious eyes. Our traditions generate lots of infirmities for they make the Word non-effective (Mk. 7:13).

We don't manufacture groaning

One of the ways the Holy Spirit helps us in prayer is through groaning. We are not making this up. We are not trying to be sensational. It is not an act initiated by our own will. A fellow who tries to pray by groaning as an act of the will is simply theatrical, if not altogether silly. When the Holy Spirit supplies the urge to groan, it tends to happen when the presence of God is manifest and the degree of infirmity is intense, when there is a crisis or grave danger to soul or physical life. In fact, the more the unbelief in the person that we are praying for or the more the resistance presented, we find that the groanings increase. They are the expression of the handicap experienced.

We yield to these groanings for that's what the occasion demands. We pray with groanings, until the urge to groan stops. We know we have the victory. We give God praise.

It is not important to groan. What is important is responding to whatever the Spirit supplies to us in prayer.

Birthing in prayer

My little children, of whom I travail in birth again until Christ be formed in you,
Galatians 4:19

Paul travailed in birth until the sinners in Galatia received the Gospel and became Christians. Travail sometimes comes with intense groanings, as a woman would in childbirth. It tends not to be the case that women are sipping ice cream and giggling while giving birth.

We do not manufacture spiritual travail; we just yield to it when the Lord gives it. This is the spiritual meaning of "as soon as Zion travailed....". The church is referred to as Zion (Heb. 12:22-23). Children are birthed spiritually first in intercessory prayer and then we give them the Word which they receive into their hearts by believing the gospel. They don't receive our groaning nor are they required to groan. When we rise up from the place of groaning, we can rest assured that as someone preaches reconciliation to them their heart is more open to the Word.

We are led into interceding for people this way because their hearts have been blinded by satan.

It also tends to be the case that whenever the number of unbelievers in a meeting would be much as is the case in an evangelistic meeting, the tendency to pray by groaning increases too. This intensifies when the altar call is given. Most unlearned believers take it to mean that they need to get "born again" again. In reality they are sensing the compassion that brings supernatural deliverance to those who are in bondage. They can yield to that compassion by praying in the Spirit.

Don't be a distraction

The compassion of Jesus has been misunderstood. What is happening at those times is that the Lord Jesus through the Holy Spirit is distributing the feeling of the infirmity of blindness of heart for the believers in that congregation to take hold of and pray off.

This feeling starts in the spirit, for it comes through the Holy Spirit who is a spirit. It later registers in our soul but compassion did not start there. Instead of responding to the compassion of the Lord by praying for the lost, saints present at the meeting run to the altar while the sinners stay in their seats confused by all the pandemonium. The saints should pray under their breath trusting that the sinners will respond to the wooing of God's love. If you think you are going to create a scene, excuse yourself and go find a place to pray until the urgency wears off and the peace of God overwhelms your heart.

At those times our Father God is not requiring you to get born-again again. You already belong to Him and He knows that. He wants someone smart enough to use the authority of their humanity to pray so spiritual babies can be born.

Once again, this kind of praying might be accompanied by a groan. Since we are wise people we know that such groaning is best done, as we stay sensitive to God before the unbelievers come to our meetings. The Lord Jesus would have given us inside information by the Holy Spirit in advance. If we stay sensitive to Him and He gives us a burden, we would pray with tongues and groanings before our meetings. When these unbelievers arrive, it is time to harvest them.

Groaning in front of the world is silly. You might confirm that you are a nut case, become the attraction for the meeting and everyone goes home entertained but no spiritual new-born babies were born.

Feeling what God feels about human feelings

Divine compassion is of the spirit for it originates in God who is a spirit.

The compassion of the Lord destroys bondage.

When we get ourselves cornered into a tight spot the Lord Jesus in heaven is touched with the feeling of our infirmity (Heb. 4:15) in the spirit.

Divine compassion in the Lord Jesus is transmitted by the Spirit of God and passes through our reborn human spirits until it registers in our hearts. We begin to identify with what Jesus feels about the feelings of men.

Divine compassion is not about looking at men and feeling their infirmities, it is linking up with the Lord Jesus by the Holy Ghost in our own spirits. We feel what God feels about the feelings of men.

Compassion registers in our emotions but is not emotional.

But whoso hath this world's good, and seeth his brother have need, and shutteth up his bowels of compassion from him, how dwelleth the love of God in him?
1 John 3:17

Notice that the believer can shut up his own bowels of compassion. Thus our fleshly choices can shut down compassion from flowing from our spirits into our hearts and out into the lives of people who need it.

It is as we walk in love and maintain a tender heart that this free flow of compassion intensifies.

One of the characteristics of a tender heart is that it does not rejoice when tragedy befalls people who have been evil themselves. Even if people are evil and wicked, we know who we are. We are of God. We are like our Lord; we are moved with compassion and not by bitterness (See Lk. 7:13).

11

PRAYER OF INTERCESSION

God is not angry with men

At the birth of Jesus, the angels declared, "Glory to God in the highest, and on earth peace, goodwill towards men" (Lk 2:14)

Though what those angels declared has been repeated in countless Christmas sermons, dramas and plays, the wonder of its message is still lost on many Christians. We think God is angry with man but that is not true.

The message of those angels was not goodwill amongst men, which would have made it more of a United Nations political declaration. It does not even mean that nations will stop fighting one another.

What it means is that always flowing from God towards man

is goodwill. Man did not know this therefore God sent those angels to declare it. To prove His goodwill, God was becoming a baby that very night. Surely by becoming man God was telling us he was comfortable as a man. Jesus was not silently cursing under His breath as a man, He loved every minute of it. God does not consider becoming a man to be a downgrade.

What a shame it is that we do not know what it is to be a man; therefore we do not enjoy being men. We want to be other than man.

God did not have a change of mind towards man. Man is God's idea. Those angels were not announcing that God was no longer angry and that He had softened towards man at last. God had goodwill towards man but without men that would showcase God's heart, God was working within tight parameters within which He could express it. There were things He could start saying because of the birth of that champion from heaven – Jesus! The boiling anger of God causes Him to expose, challenge, dismantle and heal the ungodliness of ungodly men while He unconditionally loves those men.

As good as the message of goodwill from those angels were, there is something that is much more than the declaration of those angels. The Lord Jesus has actually been made the propitiation for all sins both that of saints and sinners (1 John 2:2). Jesus is the basis on which God shows mercy.

When men have been their vilest and you want to pray for them, as you approach God in prayer, upgrade your thoughts from dwelling on the vileness of their actions and instead fill your hearts with the heroic love of Jesus. Remember Jesus.

God is already merciful

But if our gospel be hid, it is hid to them that are lost: In whom the god of this world hath blinded the minds of them which believe not, lest the light of the glorious gospel of Christ, who is the image of God, should shine unto them.
2 Corinthians 4:3-4

Religious thinking has drilled it into our psyche that the issue is that God is angry at men; therefore, He holds back His mercy. We think that if God showed more mercy the world would be some utopia and the lives of the people we are praying for would change dramatically. We think it is a deficiency of God's mercy that is the problem. So we set ourselves in intercession to make Him show mercy instead of anger. In reality, God does not need to be more merciful nor can He afford to be. Jesus is the rain that God sends upon the just and unjust. If God needs to show more mercy, where would He get it? There is no mercy greater than Christ Jesus.

The reason for intercession today

The reason for the prayer of intercession is because satan blinds men to the truth of the gospel, therefore, they do not see the light of who God is and what His love has done in redemption. This blindness causes them to reject the truth without really hearing it properly.

They have been encouraged to think God is the problem when they have heard religious people tell them, "God is mad at you because you did such and such a thing". Unconsciously, the church is the avenue through which people become blinded to God's true nature. We think we are teaching holiness, whereas we are just blinding people to the reconciliation that God has provided in Christ. If you don't want to have to pray the prayer of intercession for your kids when they grow up, stop telling them in their childhood years that God is mad at them when they are naughty. Speak God's blessing over them because Jesus is the basis of mercy and the foundation of grace.

We don't intercede because God is angry. When people persist in sin, God does not hold back His mercy; instead, it is people that forsake their own mercies! (Jonah 2:8). We intercede because people are sowing and reaping satanic destruction. Where intercession deals with God's mercy, we thank Him profusely because He freely shows mercy because Jesus is the propitiation for all sin.

People who are blinded by satan cooperate with satan to co-create calamity for themselves and for others. There is a whole lot of "mess" to be reaped unless someone stands in between people and the alliance they have formed with satan through ignorance.

Intercession defined

The prayer that we pray to suspend the advantage satan has over people through ignorance and blindness is the prayer of intercession. They are sowing to the flesh and reaping judgment. Through intercession, we are holding back the judgment that men draw upon themselves because of their blind minds.

Our primary aim in praying the prayer of intercession today is to respond to God who is love, by sensing and responding to God's love within us (See Rom. 5:5).

The redemption that we have in Christ Jesus has radically

changed the nature of intercession. The Old Testament saints did not have Jesus; in the day of the New Covenant we do. Therefore, the way Moses, Abraham and the Old Testament saints prayed and the way we pray the prayer of intercession are radically different.

Though people sinned then and they still sin today, there is a big difference – His name is Jesus.

The Bible contains examples of intercessors before Jesus came.

Abraham was a limited Mediator

And the LORD said, Because the cry of Sodom and Gomorrah is great, and because their sin is very grievous; I will go down now, and see whether they have done altogether according to the cry of it, which is come unto me; and if not, I will know. And the men turned their faces from thence, and went toward Sodom: but Abraham stood yet before the LORD. And Abraham drew near, and said, Wilt thou also destroy the righteous with the wicked? Peradventure there be fifty righteous within the city: wilt thou also destroy and not spare the place for the fifty righteous that are therein? That be far from thee to do after this manner, to slay the righteous with the wicked: and that the righteous should be as the wicked, that be far from thee: Shall not the Judge of all the earth do right? And the LORD said, If I find in Sodom fifty righteous within the city, then I will spare all the place for their sakes. And he said, Oh let not the LORD be angry, and I will speak yet but this once: Peradventure ten shall be found there. And he said, I will not destroy it for ten's sake.
Genesis 18:20, 23 - 26, 32

Sin confuses men; there is nothing good about it. As you read this story, you cannot help but notice that even though a city is sinful, God will spare that city for the sake of those who are His. Abraham did not catch that hint. His limited revelation of God's true nature limited his effectiveness in intercession.

God later showed Ezekiel that He would spare a city for the sake of one man who makes up the hedge (Ezek. 22:30). We should not be looking for reasons why a city should be destroyed but how to preserve them; in order that they might hear the Gospel and respond in faith.

In order to understand this story, remember that God gave man authority on the earth (Gen. 1:26). Man is the one that authorizes good or bad spirits to work on this earth. The Bible does not tell us anything about God creating thorns. It was Adam's actions that caused the earth to produce thorns (Gen. 3:18).

By cooperating with satan, Adam had sown violence into the earth and the earth revolted with all sorts of abominations.

In Abraham's day, a spiritual cry rose out of Sodom because men had saturated the earth with violence. It was a cry for judgment. It was like thick, dark rain clouds gathering just before it rains. Man's action was cooperating with satan and shrinking God's protective presence on earth, while giving satan access to steal, kill and destroy.

In His mercy, God was looking to use Abraham's authority to rescue Sodom by withholding judgment. God wanted to use the intercession of Abraham to bring God's protective presence to spare that land. The citizens of Sodom had by their sin and unbelief cooperated with satan and banished God's protective presence and given place to the devil who wreaked havoc and wiped out Sodom. If Sodom had repented, their repentance would have increased the footprint of God's protective presence (Ezek. 33:11).

Satan is unable to kill and destroy in an atmosphere of faith.

God does not decide which lands to spare and which to destroy. Man is the variable. Sometimes, man uses his God-given authority and through intercession invites the protective presence of God. At other times, man does not take his place. God is always looking for a man (Ezek. 22:30). Jesus is the basis for God's mercy, not our intercession. Intercession wears down the cooperation and power that men supply to satan.

Abraham did not see God

Abraham did not see God (John 1:18). Abraham did not understand God's true nature. Abraham did not know that God loved the whole world and would go to any length for the salvation of one soul. In his intercession, he did not once ask for God's mercy! He had limited understanding of how to function as an intercessor. Abraham was unsure as to how right God would be in His dealings. He wrongly assumed that God could find ten righteous people in Sodom. Abraham could only intercede on the natural plane. None of the conditions he gave God could be met.

He did not even remember Lot. Thankfully God did. In God's merciful provision, nothing could happen until Lot was safe (Gen. 19:22).

Jesus is the greater intercessor who obtained redemption for the whole world, though Abraham failed at sparing Sodom.

Moses was also a limited Mediator

Moses also functioned as a mediator (Gal. 3:19).

Reading through the Old Testament we can see that Moses often begged God not to destroy the people. He thought that God is the one that destroys men. However we now know that God is not the adversary trying to destroy man (See John 10:10). Satan is. Moses did not know these facts.

In fact, you don't find much information about satan in the writings of Moses apart from that of the serpent tempting Eve in the garden. Based on Moses' limited understanding, he saw God as the adversary who could destroy the people because they provoked Him.

> *Turn from thy fierce wrath, and repent of this evil against thy people.*
> *Exodus 32:12b*

Moses felt that God's will was wrath. Therefore, he prayed for God's will to be suspended. We now know that God is not willing that any should perish (2 Pet. 3:9). It would be incorrect to tell God to turn from His fierce wrath today!

We don't want to change God's will

New Testament prayer does not get God to alter His will. It gets us to alter ours, so that we come into alignment with God. Jesus prayed, "Your will be done on earth" (Mt. 6:10). Not once did Jesus ask that God repent of His planned evil as Moses prayed (Ex. 32:12). Jesus saw no need to change God's will. He prayed to release it. Jesus never attempted to change God's mind, He was the revelation of it.

We don't really understand intercession, by studying intercessions in the Old Testament. We understand intercession, by understanding Jesus **the intercessor**. We are to pray like Jesus, not like Moses. We pray for men today but we are conscious of the key New Testament fact that just as there is only one God, there is also only one intercessor and the position of intercessor is not up for grabs - Jesus is the only intercessor today (See 1 Tim. 2:5).

The reason for the extensive destructions in the Old Testament was neither due to those people being worse sinners nor did it have anything to do with God having anger issues. There was just no man to function as intercessor to delay the reaping of the harvest of unbelief (See Isaiah 59:16).

Solomon concluded that it was better to be dead than alive under that setup (See Eccl. 4:1-3). This is why God gave us Jesus the righteous one (See 1 Jn. 2:1).

Now that we have an Intercessor and the power of the new nature, power is no longer on the side of the oppressor! We should expect a different outcome in our day because there is a man in heaven at the right hand of God, who releases supernatural power as He prays through the church on earth.

Believers who do not understand this change that happened at the ushering in of the New Testament are trying to be intercessors supposedly holding back the fierce wrath of God. They are barking up the wrong tree however, because God is not looking for a way to condemn men. God is looking for a way to get people to see what Christ has accomplished and to walk in the knowledge of it (See 1 Tim. 2:4).

Yielding to Jesus the Intercessor

Our effectiveness in praying for others in the New Testament is directly linked to our understanding of how to cooperate with the compassion of **Jesus** who is **the** Intercessor. Jesus is not the best intercessor, He is the only intercessor. Any prayer of intercession must stay conscious of this. We are not standing between God and men trying to talk God out of sending calamity. God is not out to destroy your loved one in the first instance, even if they have sinned; therefore, your prayers cannot stop Him from doing so. We are not even telling God to show mercy! Jesus is the mercy of God. We are standing between men and their reaping the harvests of unbelief. We are weakening their cooperation with the destroyer who steals and kills. We are combating the blindness in the hearts of men, so that they can receive the light of God's Word (2 Cor. 4:3).

We cannot use prayer alone to achieve what the Lord has said is to be achieved through His Word, for God saves through the foolishness of preaching (1 Cor. 1:18). How demons must love it that we keep waiting for a move of God not realizing that we are the move of God! The truth is that Jesus is stirring us by His Word and His Spirit to act as His body and His men on the earth. We are the embodiment of Christ. We are the embodiment of power. We are to heal the sick, preach the Word and be the light of our world.

Jesus is the Intercessor

Wherefore he is able also to save them to the uttermost that come unto God by him, seeing he ever liveth to make intercession for them.
Hebrews 7:25

Jesus is now the mediator between God and man because He is also a man. Jesus is in heaven, not on the earth. All the prayers that men prayed in the Bible were prayed from the earth because the earth is man's dominion. The intercession that Jesus makes is forever. This intercession is the life that He lives for us as the representative man in the heavens, the Head of the Church. When Jesus needs to pray as the Intercessor, He cannot do so in heaven, for heaven is not man's dominion. He is touched with the feelings of our infirmities – the infirmity of blindness and ignorance. He shares these feelings as burdens that men on the earth pray off. It is important to understand this. Jesus prays through you as you yield in love to His Spirit within your reborn spirit.

And he that searcheth the hearts knoweth what is the mind of the Spirit, because he maketh intercession for the saints according to the will of God.
Romans 8:27

You'll notice that "the will of" is italicized because it was not in the original Greek but added by translators to make it more readable. Without the italics it reads, "… he maketh intercession for the saints according to God". Thus, Christ the intercessor in the heavens generates intercession within your spirit, so that you pray exactly as God would have prayed in that situation.

Jesus makes intercession through us, so that we now pray beyond our natural limitations, especially the limitation of knowledge. This way, we bypass the challenge that Abraham and Moses had due to their limited comprehension of the situation at hand. We are praying on a supernatural plane. This is what praying in tongues is really about. It is like a ladder of elevation above limitations imposed by our humanity (See author's book – The Secret Behind The Secret).

Since we are one spirit with Him (1 Cor. 6:17), the Lord Jesus by the Holy Spirit links up with our human spirits. This way, He prays out His desire as we pray in the spirit.

Jesus has comprehensive knowledge of events

New Testament prayer is cooperation between Jesus in heaven and the believer on earth through the Spirit of God. The Lord Jesus, as Intercessor at the right hand of the Father, has comprehensive insight of events. His insight penetrates into depths that our human brains do not fully grasp and many times know nothing about. He deposits the fragment of His comprehension, which we need to know, into our spirits as supernatural insight, which we then pray out.

Jesus is not actually praying in heaven right now, though He is interceding. Jesus does the prayer aspect of His intercession by praying through the recreated spirits of men on the earth. He prays through us supernaturally for it is the prayers prayed on the earth that supplies tremendous power for God to work with on earth (See Jam. 5:16).

The Lord Jesus is doing the intercession, while we are doing the praying on the basis of His intercession.

Economics of Spiritual Power

Such religious jargon is completely out of rhythm with the head. You are directly connected to Christ who like a choir conductor draws out the music in everyone like a tapestry of art that intertwines in harmony to reveal the full stature of divine inspiration (which is Christ in you.)
Colossians 2:19 (MIRROR)

And not holding the Head, from which all the body by joints and bands
having nourishment ministered, and knit together, increaseth with the
increase of God.
Colossians 2:19

The body of Christ is a nation. It has its own market forces of
supply and demand. When there is demand from one member
of the body, there has to be supply from another. We must
understand the economics of spiritual power. This deals with
how Jesus meets needs and directs resources to where it is
needed in the body of Christ.

Jesus is the head of the body and the body is the fullness of
Him. Without the body of believers on the earth He has no
fullness on the earth today.

In order for Him to be fully effective on the earth, He engages
His body of believers on the earth. There is no variableness
in Him, though there is variation in His effectiveness. This is
because there is variation in how believers respond to Him when
He brings supernatural information by the Holy Spirit to our
human spirit. If we do not yield to His prompting to pray and
He is unable to get someone else to yield to Him, He is greatly
limited in bringing to pass the manifestation of His will on
the earth. As we learn to cooperate with Jesus the intercessor,
believers begin to enjoy His power to save to the uttermost.

We often receive benefits manifested in our lives that we know
we have not necessarily believed for or even prayed about. More
often than not, it is because the Lord Jesus was able to get the
substance of the answer through to someone on the earth who
supernaturally prayed these into manifestation. The one who
prayed is not the source of the goodness, the Lord Jesus is.
The one who prayed supplied the authority for transferring the

goodness in invisible form into the earth, where a man can enjoy it. There are things within the plan of the Lord Jesus as the Head of the church for you, which you would not experience except as you learn to respond to the promptings of the indwelling Spirit.

If the believer who was given a prompting knows what the prompting is about and he knows how to scripturally pray about such, he can pray in his understanding and usher in the intended results of Jesus the intercessor. If however, the believer has a prompting but is unclear as to what the situation is about or how to pray for it effectively, the best response is to pray in tongues. That kind of praying bypasses the limitations of our brain. The believer on the earth does not even need to know what the situation is about. As we yield our authority to Jesus the Intercessor, we are able to usher in the manifestation of supernatural deliverance for others.

Sometimes the Lord awakens us and withdraws our sleep because He wants to borrow our humanity to resolve a matter in prayer. Rather than enter into prayer, we make ourselves a hot cup of chocolate so we can bring about "sweet sleep" and thereby we successfully quench the urgency of the Spirit. We should learn to lend ourselves to Him and pray.

12

ORDER IN PRAYER

First of all

I exhort therefore, that, first of all, supplications, prayers, intercessions, and giving of thanks, be made for all men;
1 Timothy 2:1

As we pay close attention to the way these prayers have been listed, we find that God is trying to get something across to us about divine order. Some sort of order is intended because of the words, "first of all". We need to understand this.

Supplications tend to engage a lot of our soul. Prayers signify worship. Worship takes us into the spirit more than the soul. Intercession works best when we are in tune with the spirit.

Notice that all the prayers listed here are plural – supplications, prayers, intercessions and giving of thanks. They are all prayers that we can pray over and over again.

When to pray for people instead of things

Note again that all the prayers listed in this verse are for people and not for things. None of these prayers is about the moving of mountains or removal of personal hindrances. God wants us to live a quiet and peaceful life. He does not ask us to focus our prayers on receiving quiet and peace into our lives. He goes about it a different way.

It is OK to use this as the foundation for praying for political leaders. Notice that the verse has more than Presidents in mind; it actually says **all those in authority**. That is a much wider scope than just Presidents and Heads of States.

When I am in an airplane, my peace and safety as well as that of other passengers on board is more directly influenced by the pilots than by the Prime Minister of England. That pilot is the man in authority over that airplane.

These prayers are for people who have influence over a sphere of life. These people control things. Rather than pray about the things that these people have control over, we pray for them directly. If I wanted a job, I could focus on the job as a thing. Otherwise using this principle of **praying for those in authority,** I would pray for the man who rules over the interview process – the decision maker. He is a man in authority in that situation.

If my marriage were in turmoil, using this principle I would pray more for my spouse than for the thing called stable marriage. How I relate to my wife affects outcomes more than anything else.

Priorities and Patterns in prayer

I pray for them: I pray not for the world, but for them which thou hast given me; for they are thine.
John 17:9

The Lord Jesus made an Interesting point that lets us see His priorities in prayer. He said that He was praying for the saints and that He does not pray for the world. This shows that when praying for others, Jesus prioritised prayer for His saints above prayer for non-saints.

If we could observe Jesus at close quarters, we would find that based upon His pattern prayer in John 17, the large proportion of His prayers seem to be for the saints. His prayers for the lost would be fewer compared to that for saints. This is because His prayers would help nurture strong saints. These healthy saints would then influence the world. Jesus prayed more for the saints than He prayed for the world. He prayed where His own influence was stronger.

We tend to violate this concept by focusing the majority of our prayers on the lost and little time on the saints.

The Lord made further statements about His prayers for the saints.

Pray and influence

And the Lord said, Simon, Simon, behold, Satan hath desired to have you, that he may sift you as wheat: 32 But I have prayed for thee, that thy faith fail not: and when thou art converted, strengthen thy brethren.
Luke 22:32

Simon Peter was the foremost amongst the leaders that could strengthen the brethren. He was a leader of men.

Among the saints, the Lord Jesus prayed more for the leaders because they held influence over the saints. It was not only Peter that ran away from Jesus but Jesus focused His prayers on Peter. Peter held the power of leadership, which could influence the others. Jesus prayed more for the saints in leadership than He prayed for those that were not.

When Jesus sensed to pray for Peter, He did not misuse that anointing by using it to complain about Peter instead. Many times we do sense genuine impressions from the Spirit of God to pray for the saints but because we are untaught, we dissipate that impression in judgement and accusation. When we belly ache and gripe about people, we unconsciously divert God's power for the devil's use!

Unless we are schooled in how to walk in honour towards our leaders, we find that when we render service to them; we do so in the flesh, which causes us to send paralysing analysis towards them. This in turn poisons our hearts and causes us to walk dishonourably towards them.

We tend to violate this concept of praying for leaders by focusing majority of our prayers on the saints and little time on the leaders amongst the saints.

Paul shed some light along these lines when he said:

> *I exhort therefore, that, first of all, supplications, prayers, intercessions, and giving of thanks, be made for all men; For kings, and for all that are in authority; that we may lead a quiet and peaceable life in all godliness and honesty. For this is good and acceptable in the sight of God our Saviour; Who will have all men to be saved, and to come unto the*

knowledge of the truth.
1 Timothy 2:1 - 4

When praying for all men we are to especially concentrate on the kings and those in authority. These people are influencers. There are people whose decisions influence the expression of rest or unrest in large communities.

Ordinarily, we should give more attention in prayer to pray for those who are influencers amongst the kings. The pattern is to concentrate on influencers and authorities among the saints as well as the world.

Give ourselves to prayer and ministry

The smallest church is the home.

Ruling one's household well is a pre-requisite for a bishop (1 Tim. 3:1-5). A bishop who is heavy-handed with his family will be heavy handed and harsh with the flock of God. The home is the first church. You would expect that given the primal nature of the home, we should pray first for our families before we pray for our ministry. A fellow who neglects praying for his family and instead focuses exclusively on his "ministry" is not doing the first things first. Moreover he is worse than an infidel. God needs us to cooperate with Him in order for God to be able to legally bring His influence to bear in our families, in the church and on the earth.

As we stay conscious of these principles and lend our authority to the Lord in prayer, we authorize and release the power that is required to get God's will done on earth!

Keep giving yourself to that supernatural communion between

your human spirit on the earth and the Spirit of God in the spirit dimension by speaking God's words to God with your mouth and your thoughts so that God reaps intimacy of the highest order.

We Win!